Anarcho Punk
Albums

ANARCHO PUNK ALBUMS

THE BAND'S STORY BEHIND ANARCHIST PUNK MUSIC

by

Gary Miller

Contents

Foreword 1

Crass 7

Chumbawamba 15

Omega Tribe 29

Subhumans... 37

Zounds 45

Blyth Power 61

Lost Cherrees.. 67

Antisect.. 81

The Cravats... 101

Flux Of Pink Indians 109

Rubella Ballet 115

Icons Of Filth 133

Dedications And Acknowledgements................................. 153

FOREWORD

PUNK IS DEAD, LONG LIVE PUNK – Penny Rimbaud

The term 'anarcho-punk' is derived from punk rock music which promoted anarchism in all its forms and exclusively evolved around a group of bands in the late 1970s and continued into the 80s.

The first glimpse of punk promoting this ideology was the Sex Pistols and their debut single, 'Anarchy in the UK'. However, this was soon to be taken lightly and seen as more of a 'shock tactic' than any serious crusade to expound thoughtful anarchist ideology.

Crass changed all of that and saw anarchy as a way of life and a resistance to authority. They became advocates of direct action, feminism, animal rights and anti-war. Other bands were soon on the scene, such as Poison Girls, Chumbawamba, Flux of Pink Indians and Subhumans. The music varied from group to group and took punk to a different level. The emphasis shifted from the music to the message. The sleeve design of the singles and albums became just as important as the musical content itself and fully subscribed to the Do-It-Yourself ethic. As well as containing lyrics to the songs, the covers, often gatefold, held a plethora of information, illustration, and ideologies. It's where the message was indeed communicated.

"Whilst the movement soon gained momentum, it's without a doubt that Crass unknowingly (unwittingly) got the proverbial ball rolling. During 1977, in an open house community called Dial House in Essex, I started 'messing about' with Penny Rimbaud; having seen The Clash live in Bristol, I was inspired to start a band, and Penny offered to play the drums. Penny was working on his book, 'Reality Asylum', and that again inspired me to write the song 'So What'. This was followed by 'Owe Us A Living', and armed with these, we set about taking on the world as a drum and vocals outfit.

"Other Dial House attendees joined; Pete Wright on Bass, Phil Free and Andy Palmer on lead and rhythm guitars respectively. Eve Libertine performed vocals and was later joined by Joy D'vivre. We recorded 'Feeding of the 5000' and after its' release found ourselves playing hundreds of gigs to a growing audience of like-minded discontented people.

"So, anarcho-punk had begun, and other bands took up the gauntlet. As the decade moved into the 80s and Thatcher wielded her authority, the feeling of discontent magnified. Squats sprung

up everywhere, prime examples in London being Huntley Street, Brougham Road in Hackney, Gerrard Road and Cross Street in Islington. Gigs were monitored and sometimes even stopped by the police, and MI5 had many of the bands on their radar. This wasn't a few kids rebelling against authority for no particular reason; this was a movement, a fundamental shift towards a society which had left the working class behind.

"Although the music charts didn't reflect it at the time, 'anarcho-punk' was also commercially successful. Even if the money went to worthwhile causes, such as supporting the Miners, Rape Crisis Centers, Drug Addiction Clinics to name just a few, both singles and albums would sell in their thousands and often needed represses.

"The 'movement' rocked the established Music Industry and gave it a run for its' money. It's a great example of what can be achieved when like-minded souls get together – I'm so proud to have been a part of it."

Steve Ignorant – Lead Vocals, Crass

The legacy of anarcho-punk is still here today with new bands emerging (as well as a handful still performing, often in sold-out venues). Is it a coincidence that the whole political landscape is again very similar to the 80s and we have our very own Thatcher/Reagan characters playing with people's lives?

However, it was the albums of the 80s which defined the movement and the bands featured in this book are a testimony to their art. Read the book while cranking up the volume and listening to the featured albums. They all sound just as good today.

anarchy

[an-er-kee]

noun

1. a state of society without government or law

2. political and social disorder due to the absence of governmental control

3. anarchism (def 1).

4. lack of obedience to an authority; insubordination

5. confusion and disorder

Synonyms: chaos, disruption, turbulence, disorganization, disintegration

punk

[puhngk]

noun

1. a type of rock-n-roll, reaching its peak in the late 1970s and characterised by loud, insistent music and abusive or violent protest lyrics, and whose performers and followers are distinguished by extremes of dress and socially defiant behaviour

CRASS
THE FEEDING OF THE 5000

No book, no blog, no conversation regarding anarcho-punk would be complete without the mention of Crass. Formed during 1977, the band promoted anarchism as a way of life and a political ideology. They advocated direct action, animal rights, feminism and used art in all its forms to publicise their message. The police and even MI5 were keen observers, and they posed a significant threat to the government; their record sales often outselling the household names of the pop world. Crass was the real deal when it came to anarcho-punk, and although they would never admit it themselves, they were the catalyst for the whole movement.

Based around Dial House, a farm cottage situated in South West Essex, co-founder, Penny Rimbaud, began jamming with Steve Ignorant who was living at the house at the time. We asked Penny how Crass were formed.

"Organically. People passed through Dial House where Steve (Ignorant) and myself lived, and some of them liked what was happening and wanted to join in. Some of them helped in the garden. Some of them baked bread. Some of them sat around reading books from our extensive library. Some of them just enjoyed doing nothing, and some of them joined Steve and me in creating a noise which eventually became known as Crass."

So what, so what
So what if Jesus died on the cross
So what about the fucker, I don't give a toss
So what if the master walked on the water
I don't see him trying to stop the slaughter
They say I wouldn't have to live from bins
If I would go along, confess my sins
They say I shouldn't commit no crime
'Cause Jesus Christ is watching all the time

Steve Ignorant (born Steve Williams) had been keen to form a band after seeing The Clash live in Bristol where singer Joe Strummer professed, "If you think you can do it better, start your own band." Fully intending to do just that, Steve returned to Dial House, where he had initially visited during his early teens, and started writing new material with Penny who explains, in his own inimitable way, about those first years.

"Early years? Things happen of their own accord. I've always been an artist of some sort or another; writer, painter, musician. I never really know what any day might bring, and I never have. One day a gardener, the next a poet. I guess it all depends on what needs doing and I guess I could say that I've always followed that path. There's no point in writing a poem if there's no point in doing so. As I say, things just happened."

Penny had already written 'Reality Asylum', an outlandish condemnation of Christ, the martyr, which would later be banned from the opening track on 'Feeding of the 5000' after the Irish record manufacturers refused to handle it. 'Reality Asylum' was replaced on the album by two minutes of silence and renamed 'The Sound of Free Speech'. This also prompted Crass to set up their self-titled record label soon after to take full control of their material.

Steve Ignorant wrote 'So What?' and 'Do They Owe Us a Living?' as a drum and vocal duo before other Dial House friends, Gee Vaucher, Pete Wright, Andy Palmer and Steve Herman joined the band. Herman left soon after and was replaced by Phil Clancey (better known as Phil Free) on guitar while Joy D'vivre and Eve Libertine joined around the same time.

Crass starting gigging more, regularly with UK Subs, although the original audiences were small. They played two gigs at the Roxy Club in Covent Garden, London, where they turned up drunk for the second show and were ejected from the stage during the performance. This was the inspiration behind 'Banned from the Roxy', a stand out track on the soon to be released debut album.

Banned from the Roxy... OK

I never much liked playing there, anyway

They said they only wanted well-behaved boys

Do they think guitars and microphones are just fucking toys?

Fuck 'em, I've chosen to make my stand

Against what I feel is wrong with this land

They just sit there on their overfed arses

Feeding off the sweat of less fortunate classes

Crass began to take themselves more seriously as it became apparent that they were onto something unlike anything which had proceeded them, their audiences had grown thus. A debut album was on the horizon, an eighteen track, 12", 45rpm EP, but who's idea was it and who wrote the material?

"It just happened," says Penny. "We'd written something around fifteen songs. Small Wonder Records wanted to put out a single by Crass and asked what song we would like to release. We said that we'd like to release all of them, so that's what we did. It was the first ever multi-track, 45rpm, 12" single. Tough for those many people who played it at 33rpm without knowing!

"It was a joint effort. Our only rule was that if someone didn't like something, we didn't do it. No discussion, we simply didn't do it," continues drummer Rimbaud, "there were no rows, no disagreements. Why would we want to do it if it was going to lead to discomforts? Pete, the bassist, had a very different idea of timing to myself. His idea of, say, the fourth beat was not mine nor, I might say, of anyone else I know. But hey, what's in a beat?"

'Feeding of the 5000' was considered revolutionary at the time of release. The sound hadn't been heard before and coupled with the blasphemous lyrics and political ideology, the album is regarded as the first to promote thoughtful anarchist attitude.

"The intent was to say it as we saw it. If that shocked and angered people, then that was their problem which they could either sort out or not. If what we said shook people out of 'their' lethargy, then that's no bad thing, but I don't think that was our intent. As I said, we simply said it as we saw it. It's something that I still do," adds Penny.

Did Crass invent anarcho-punk though?

"Anarcho-punk was a media invention to separate that which had meaning and positive intent from the commercial pap which served the interests of the status quo. The term was used to isolate us from the mainstream, to lessen our social effect. At one time, Crass were far outselling any of the commercial punk bands (Pistols, Clash etc.), but the charts no more reflected this than did the music press. What does that tell us? It tells us that what we hear from the mass media is highly controlled from above.

One of our most diligent followers were MI5. Now then, that's some fan base."

The album name came about as 5000 was the minimum number of records Small Wonder Records would press, although Penny thought it was around 4900 too many. However, sales and stories were never his things.

"There were lots of stories around at the time, but no one's going to hear them, partly because I can't remember them and partly because if I can't remember them, they can't be worth hearing. In any case, Crass were engaged in making meaningful statements; stories weren't our line. And what's more, 'Hello Magazine' never offered to run an exclusive."

Almost forty years after the initial release of 'Feeding of the 5000', the world still finds itself in a state of disillusionment, but even now, Penny has his ideas about what we should do.

"What's new about there being a lot of disillusionment around and the country being a shit place to be? It's just the same now as it was then. The political issue at the time and the political issue now is 'what are you, I, we going to do about it?' Sitting around complaining about what a bad deal we're getting pretty much ensures that we'll go on getting it. It's your life, make something of it – there is no authority but yourself.

"It's in the nature of the world to go in circles both around the sun and around our heads. Of course, the album is still relevant today, which isn't to say that

I necessarily agree with everything it says. Equally, what was appropriate action then is not necessarily appropriate now. The world goes around and around to give us endless chances to get to grips with it, to rethink ourselves, to rework our agenda, to arrive at some genuinely workable solution. Then and only then will the world stop going around our heads in circles. Then and only then will there be peace."

Whatever the thoughts of the music or the lyrics, it is without a doubt that Crass and 'Feeding of the 5000' will go down as the beginning of the anarcho-punk movement. Groundbreaking and utterly irresistible, which turned heads, not only amongst the punk community, but the country as a whole. This was an album that changed punk rock as we know it.

So, what else does Penny remember of the time?

"Cigarettes were less than £1 per twenty (I think). Good coffee was impossible to find anywhere in the UK except the Café Roma in London's Soho. Flared trousers had just gone out of fashion. The Daily Mirror was still a reasonably readable newspaper. McDonald's hadn't arrived (or if they had, no one had particularly noticed). Facebook didn't exist, and neither did laptops and smartphones. You couldn't buy vegan Doc Martens.

"Oh, and my Mum didn't much like Crass, and my father loathed it."

The Feeding of the 5000

Released 1979 – Small Wonder Records

Track Listing

1. Asylum
2. Do They Owe Us a Living?
3. End Result
4. They've Got a Bomb
5. Punk is Dead
6. Reject of Society
7. General Bacardi
8. Banned from the Roxy
9. G's Song
10. Fight War, Not Wars
11. Women
12. Securicor
13. Sucks
14. You Pay
15. Angels
16. What a Shame
17. So What
18. Well?...Do They?

CHUMBAWAMBA

PICTURES OF STARVING CHILDREN SELL RECORDS

Having formed in 1982, Chumbawamba were at the forefront of the 1980s anarcho-punk movement. Their career, spanning over three decades, oversaw a shift in musical ideas and influences but they always had that political overtone and irreverent attitude towards authority.

The initial years were convoluted while the band established itself. By the end of 1982, Lou Watts, Alice Nutter, and Dunstan Bruce had joined Boff Whalley and Danbert Nobacon, with Harry Hamer and Dave 'Mavis' Dillon linking up soon after.

Boff explains, "We'd been playing and rehearsing seriously for maybe two or three years, playing here, there and everywhere at benefit gigs, going on demonstrations, getting arrested numerous times, steadily working out how we could be a band as well as a bunch of activists. Our game plan seemed to be, basically, to enjoy ourselves, have a laugh, and at the same time break the law as much as possible!

"We lived in a squat in West Leeds. We were having the time of our lives, doing part-time jobs while signing on the dole, sharing our money and living as a collective. And we loved being part of this gang, a musical, political, piss-taking gang. Loved being part of an anarcho-punk scene, with its Do-it-Yourself ethos, while at the same time trying hard to be different from other bands."

During 1985, Chumbawamba released their first single, 'Revolution' on Agit-Prop Records, which soon sold out of its initial run and re-pressed reaching number four in the UK Indie Chart, staying there for an amazing 34 weeks. This achievement in itself could easily have been the highlight of Boff Whalley's career.

"We made a single, eventually, saving up our money to put it out. John Peel played it and, having grown up listening to and learning from his shows; it seemed like the pinnacle of what we could have achieved as a band. And maybe now, writing this thirty years later, it was. I'd be happy with that."

'Revolution' was followed during early 86 with a joint released 7" called 'We Are the World?'.

"We made another single with an American hardcore anarcho band called A State Of Mind, lovely people, bad tattoos, spiky haircuts," jokes Boff, before plans were put in place for their debut album, 'Pictures of Starving Children Sell Records', or so they thought.

Boff continues, "Then we thought, *we should do an album*'. By this time, we'd been playing concerts with Flux of Pink Indians. They had a record label called Spiderleg, and we discussed the idea of recording an album for it. When I say 'discussed', I mean it was talked about and talked about and talked about, and nothing ever happened. We used to stay at their house, we did a benefit tour for the miners during the 1984 strike with Flux and KUKL, limping around the country in a knackered bus. They were great people, but they didn't have the wherewithal (or the money probably) to put out our proposed album."

However, Chumbawamba were determined. "A year later, frustrated by the fact that Flux hadn't invited us down to some nice London studio to record the album, we decided to record and release it on our own. It was to be a gathering of the songs and ideas we'd been playing live over the past couple of years. We had the songs, and we just about knew how to play our instruments. Sorted."

The album was coming together nicely when an unfortunate event altered all previous plans.

"We booked a studio, a local studio where we'd recorded our first single, in Castleford, Yorkshire. We chose it because The Instigators had told us it had a brilliant engineer [Neil Ferguson]. They were right. Then three weeks before we were due to go in the studio, Bob Geldof announced, 'Live Aid'!" exclaims Boff.

Most of the music and lyrics were already in place, with around ten songs in place to record but Live Aid changed everything.

"I'd been on a course at the WEA (Workers Educational Association) learning about world politics, about charity and how it works. And the idea that all these rock stars were going to get together to solve the problems of hunger and starvation was a catalyst for us all re-thinking the album we were about to make. What about if we scrap the songs we have – that we know so well, that we love – and re-write them, so they're all about this Live Aid concert?

"And basically, that's what we did. We scrapped our history of songs and lyrics and made an album all about charity, change and the politics of starvation. We used all sorts of ways of saying what we wanted to say musically. Folk, rock, punk, dance beats, whatever. We were prepared to plunder it all to make an album that tried to argue a political point in an entertaining way."

'Pictures of Starving Children' certainly introduced Chumbawamba onto the anarcho-punk stage and was a defining moment in their history. Many punks didn't agree that this was indeed 'punk' (but who decides what is?). It was tuneful and certainly as innovative as anything that proceeded it but contained lyrics as hard-hitting, and damned relevant, as any other anarcho-punk album ever recorded. This wasn't the 'norm', but quite frankly, it was a breath of fresh air and proved punk could be found in any guise as long as the message was just as strong.

"We could never have been an Antisect or a Discharge," clarifies Boff. "We had no musical plan, we couldn't play our instruments well enough (apart from Harry, our incredible drummer). Our program was to attack and subvert, to take the piss, to enjoy ourselves making music we loved, whatever genre it was. 'Pictures' sums this idea up – it's all over the place musically, it's both po-faced and silly. But it had an idea, a concept, a gathering-point.

"The album was fairly well-recorded (thanks in no small part to engineer Neil Ferguson), and we brought in keyboards and strings to balance the loud guitars and thumping snare. We were getting better at singing harmonies, too, contrasting the barked lead vocals with three-part backing vocals. Basically having a go at all the music we listened to!"

Now recording was complete, Chumba had to come up with a relevant title and cover design to capture the whole political message while maintaining the disparity of other punk albums released previously.

Boff enlightens us further, "We made the album and then had a laugh deciding on the title – how irreverent could we make it? We had the idea of calling it 'Pictures of Starving Children Sell Records' but making the title text dominant and have a tiny photograph of a starving child in the corner – partly obscured by a price tag. We were seeing how far we could take this idea, being almost obscenely, blatantly offensive while at the same time avoiding the black-and-white cut-up stencil look of many anarcho-punk albums. In contrast to the album's profoundly political theme, we deliberately chose a colour scheme of pink and grey to mirror the 1980s fetish for the Habitat palette of muted tints."

So, punk, folk, rock or wherever 'Pictures' sat in the punk spectrum, this album was indeed innovational and launched Chumbawamba as one of the most influential bands who had forthright views on many issues, including feminism, homophobia, class struggles, and anti-fascism.

Boff takes us on a track by track account of what lay behind each song.

How to Get Your Band on Television

"We'd done a few gigs with a band from the North East called Reality Control. Proper punk band. They were great. They had a song based on a TV game show, so when they split up, we nicked the idea and developed it into Slag Aid. It was a handy song to have because playing live, we could change the characters in the song depending on who was in the news.

"We were influenced by early Frank Zappa records; the way songs ran into each other and didn't behave like neat three-minute songs with typical structures etc."

British Colonialism and the BBC

"This song sounds now like a textbook reader about charity and media, a direct commentary on the stuff that was all over the television surrounding Live Aid. The middle bit about *"TV tells us what to do"* was from an earlier song we played live called 'If

You Want to Turn Me On, Turn Your Television On'.

"Lots of conga-playing here. Harry was an incredible drummer, he tied everything up rhythmically and made us sound relatively competent musicians."

Commercial Break

"Alice in character. The tune came from an earlier song that we ditched, but I can't remember the original now. This album was a Stalinist revision of our live set, we plundered all the good tunes and re-wrote new lyrics to fit. We were always on the look-out for 'characters', trying to make the live gig into something more like a theatre. We grew up in the television age and were aware that visuals stick in your memory. So right from the beginning, we did characters and visual stuff.

"At very early gigs Danbert would strip off and paint himself red while singing. We had washing lines full of washing that we strung up. Midge played the guitar with a (home-made) TV set on his head. We stuck out like a sore thumb in the anarcho-punk world, which is how we wanted it. The first time I saw Crass in a village hall in Kent I was aware of it as a piece of theatre. The lights at the front foot of the stage shining upwards into their faces, the all-black clothes, the wall-to-wall banners – it was a spectacle. That's what we aspired to, to create a spectacle."

I'm the wife of the boss of the company

And I always make my husband answer to me

But what he says about the blacks, I totally agree

The main problem is, they're not civilised, you see

Look at the way they squabble between themselves

Rioting at funerals – they'll surely go to hell

If you gave them nice houses, they'd only burn them down

You don't get that in a white man's town

And boycotting products won't do them any good

You see they need the trade to help buy food

And when I visit my niece on her beautiful homestead

The blacks who work for her seem really quite content

So I'll agree with my husband – let things stay as they are

That's always been his motto, and we've gone far

Unilever

"Almost a pop song, or as near as we got to pop in those days. It was based on Mave's bassline. I remember him playing the bass riff, and then us working out which chords would fit over it. The melody came quickly I think. This became a really popular live song; it's got a sing-along chorus. We didn't write purposely to make things poppy or catchy; it's just how our songs came out. I grew up listening to my Dad's Beatles records, so I loved melody and harmony.

"The slow bit at the end of this is Mave singing with Lou. I remember doing this in the studio, seeing how ridiculously 'smooth' we could make it so it contrasted with what had come before it and so that we could have the punchline that stopped it, which was a recording of Dan being sick in the toilet at the studio. It was all planned, and mic'd up, he took in a jar of vegetable oil to drink that would force him to throw up."

More Whitewashing

"I like this one, straight from the night classes I was taking in Leeds about world economic food policies and the politics of hunger. Blimey, I took it seriously! The classes were by the Workers Education Authority, free adult classes. Brilliant, I've got a lot to thank them and their teachers for.

"We loved making songs that revolved around simple three-chord structures but had all sorts of melodies winding around them. And we were starting to really enjoy singing harmonies. It was stuff that a lot of anarcho-punk wasn't doing so we wanted to try it.

"Then of course because the tune was catchy, we'd suddenly change course and get loud, and there is Alice in fighting mood. Hunger put the sparkle back in television..."

And if you send a little money you can sleep tonight

Or starve in sympathy on a Limmits Diet

And you know that charity cures malnutrition

And hunger put the sparkle back in television

Hunger put the sparkle back in television

Hunger put the sparkle back in television

An Interlude: Beginning to Take It Back

"Typical how we didn't name the songs in a way they'd be recognisable! This song was just called Sandanista in the live set. One of our first acoustic songs, we'd done some acoustic stuff during the miners' strike, but this is when we decided to stick stuff on an album. We loved goading Maximum RocknRoll magazine into saying we "weren't punk". An accordion solo too! Must've been mad. We wrote this cos it seemed absurd that all the pop stars on television were raising money for people who were starving while the US military was fighting an ideological colonial war against starving peasants in South America."

Dutiful Servants and Political Masters

"We used this piece of music at least three times for different songs. I don't know why we just liked the chord progression. Starts with Danbert doing one of his characters and jumps into Alice and Harry yelling their heads off. With a dog bark that was recorded and then punched in by hand, in time with the beat. Sampling before samplers. That's our dog Derek; he was named affectionately after Derek Birkett, bassist of Flux of Pink Indians."

A dog stares into a gramophone trumpet, waits for its call to action

Mute and obedient, standing to attention

Look a little closer, the dog is a woman

She's working under a system that she can't understand

Trapped inside a world of labour and heat

So that she and her children will be able to eat

The trumpet is patriarchy, it's old and fixed

Where poor men are lured by desire to be rich

Where the limited power is still given to men

Where development aid is so wastefully spent

Where western education enforces this crap

Where women work in the open, yet live in a trap

There's one solution, and this is it

The dog leaps on the gramophone and has a shit

Coca-Colanisation

"An instrumental, almost, apart from a loop of DJ Tony Blackburn at the end. Experimenting with trumpets and ska beats. We rarely played instrumentals. Well, we had three lead vocalists, so it would have meant a lot of hanging around. And at the time we would have probably thought that instrumentals were a bit self-indulgent. Harry, our drummer, took a leaf out of Ringo Starr's book by refusing ever to play a drum solo."

...And in a Nutshell

"Lou singing. This is a slowed-down version of an earlier song on the album. We always enjoyed the slower things because they gave everything some light against the shade, we loved a Dutch band called The Ex who really played with that loud/quiet tension, and we tried to use it a lot, too. People later tended to think Nirvana had originated the idea, but it came more directly from Pixies, Fugazi and The Ex. I know Fugazi were big fans of The Ex."

Invasion

"The bass line on this was directly influenced by basslines played by The Alternative from Scotland; they had a single out on Crass Records, they played dead fast but had these little arpeggio basslines that gave it all some melody underneath. Actually, a fair few anarcho-punk bands did the same thing; the guitars were so distorted and overdriven that it was the bassline that carried the tune.

"I remember us having discussions about the quieter section in the middle with its emphasis on the off-beat keyboard. Some people weren't keen on the keyboard sound; it was too poppy and cute. But I think it worked if only because other people in the bands we played with weren't doing this sort of thing.

"This song and the album that followed emphasise how the backbone of some of the music was Harry's drumming and Mave's bass. If I remember rightly, they used to play together in our basement a lot and come up with little riffs that could be repeated over and over again. Then it was relatively easy to pile all our other stuff on the top, the melodies and harmonies and choruses and characters etc.

"And the end is the thing we tended to do best at the time, which was sing something revolutionary in as sweet and disarming a way as possible."

As Boff reiterates: "To me, the album is a perfect follow-up to the anarcho-punk scene it grew out of. It was both part of that scene (in being defiantly anarchist, made by a collective etc.) and a challenge to it – our use of pop and folk as well as all the guitar / shouty stuff was our way of extending the reach of anarcho-punk. Our way of saying that these anarchist ideas are applicable to all of society, and you don't have to wear black or love intense metal guitar music.

"Mind you; I still wear black all the time!"

Pictures of Starving Children Sell Records

Released 1986 – Agit-Prop Records

Track Listing

1.   How to Get Your Band on Television

2.   British Colonialism and the BBC

3.   Commercial Break

4.   Unilever

5.   More Whitewashing

6.   An Interlude: Beginning to Take It Back

7.   Dutiful Servants and Political Masters

8.   Coca-Colanisation

9.   …And in a Nutshell

10. Invasion

OMEGA TRIBE
NO LOVE LOST

Melodic anarcho-punk band Deadly Game was formed in New Barnet, London, during the summer of 1981. They soon changed their name to Omega Tribe even before they had started gigging later that same year and consisted of the following line-up;

Hugh Vivian – Guitar/Vocals

Daryl Hardcastle – Bass

Pete Shepherd – Drums.

Their second ever gig was no mean feat, supporting The Meteors at the 100 Club in London.

It was evident that Omega Tribe were gathering pace from a very early stage and during 1982, they recorded their first demo (in Poison Girls basement), which found its way to Crass, who then selected the song 'Nature Wonder' for their infamous compilation 'Bullshit Detector Two'. Crass were to have a huge influence on Omega Tribe, and the bands had met previously because Daryl was to interview them for his fanzine 'The

Realities of Society'. They also met and recruited guitarist Pete Fender (son of Poison Girls frontwoman Vi Subversa) the same year.

With the new line-up complete, they soon released their first EP, 'Angry Songs', which was produced by Penny Rimbaud and Fender on Crass Records. The single proved to be the catalyst reaching the top five of the Indie charts on release week beating the likes of The Damned, and soon many tours followed, especially with good friends Conflict.

Later in 1983, the album 'No Love Lost' was recorded but had it ever been planned?

"No. Not at all" explains Hugh. "We went to Corpus Christi to record a planned second EP, and they said why don't you do an album instead? We said 'Ok'. It was going to be Corpus Christi's second album release after, erm, I can't remember [edit: it was 'Time to See Who's Who' by Conflict] and Corpus Christi was supposed to be the bit that Crass Records wasn't, where you could do your own thing."

Daryl takes over, "Yeah, you were supposed to be able to do your own thing, but we had a massive argument about how they wanted us to record it, and we just said 'no'. However, Dan (Pete Fender) argued our case, and we ended up doing it the way we had intended."

Man made selfishness, man made possessions
Man made greed, man made oppressions
Man made government, man made war
Life is for living
Freedom's what life is for!

The album had a fresh feel to it and was highly regarded amongst the best albums to emerge from the anarcho-punk movement. Omega Tribe wanted to avoid the 'heavy thrash sound' and play the way they wanted.

"It was just how we played," insists Hugh. "It wasn't a conscious decision to play that way; it was just our style."

"It was Dan as well," quips Daryl. "He didn't just want to record a bloody noise, did he?"

"Yes, he was very good at harmonies, and stuff and the songs just lent themselves to that," confirms Hugh.

"Yeah, God knows what would have happened if we'd done it a different way with somebody else, the whole thing could have been well different," adds Daryl.

The album was not only renowned for its more melodic style, but the combination of the hard-hitting lyrics covering subjects from war to capitalism.

"Daryl wrote the majority, and I did some too," says Hugh.

Daryl leaves us in no doubt about what the major grievance was.

"The fucking government, the government cunts!"

Hugh takes a more retrospective view. "The big thing at the time was CND which was a big movement, a huge movement. At the time, there were big marches, big, big events which just don't happen anymore. Other than that, the grievances have got worse over the years. You've got war and everything and the globalisation of war for profit which is so much worse now than it was when the album came out."

If that's the case, then do the band think 'No Love Lost' would sell as well today?

"I guess if people could kind of relate to it all still, then I can't see why not. I think some of it now feels a little lyrically naïve, but that's just a maturity thing, isn't it?" Hugh replies.

"Well we were young when we wrote it and at the time punk was such a massive thing, but now there are so many different styles," adds Daryl.

Hugh adds, "That's certainly true & that's one of the major differences between that era and now is that now it's much more about specific scenes and bands don't have such a strong sense of identity or politics attached to things."

They make profit from your love, from your
possessions

They make profit from your colour, from your
confessions

They make profit from their god and profit with
their lies

They make profit from your living and profit when
you die

Back to the album, there's an interesting story behind the sleeve design as Daryl enlightens us.

"Joe Cliff (a hippy friend from Barnet) came up with the idea for the artwork with the hands and the butterflies, and Peter Shepherd (Omega Tribe original drummer) drew the artwork using his then girlfriend's hands as a model. His girlfriend was Karen Webster who now lives in Ireland and works as a teacher. When it was going to be an EP, it was going to be in full colour but as soon as we knew it was going to be an album it had to be in black and white." It's a punk thing.

'No Love Lost' certainly had a significant influence on many followers of the anarcho-punk movement at the time. Did Omega Tribe think that they and other punk bands at the time could make a difference?

"I think they thought they really could make a difference," admits Hugh.

"Yeah, definitely you thought you could make a difference. It does make a difference though, I listen to Crass, and it's made me a completely different person because I listen to them and it has made a difference to me. Crass & Poison Girls will always be my two favourite bands......ever," adds Daryl.

"I liked The Astronauts and Zounds. I think music supports people in what they think and feel and it gives people a reference point and proves they are not alone in what they are thinking. It brings people closer together," says Hugh.

Daryl explains why he thinks Omega Tribe were held in such high esteem.

"I wrote a lot of the songs that sounded a bit like Crass while Hugh wrote a lot of the songs that didn't sound like Crass but were beautiful and the combination made it a really unusual thing. Usually, you have one person who writes the songs, and everything sounds like that, but it's an amalgamation of two different things which makes it unusual."

Daryl continues, "We've always meant it. We've not meant it in all our lives...it's from the heart. We're not just a band who goes 'nah, nah, nah, nah' and then fucks off home. There's real motivation behind it."

"Yes," says Hugh, "there's *real* motivation behind it."

No Love Lost

Released 1983 – Corpus Christi Records

Track Listing

1. Duty Calls
2. Profit
3. Aftermath
4. Freedom
5. What the Hell
6. Mother of Cultivation
7. My Tears
8. Nature Wonder
9. Pictures
10. Man Made
11. My Tears Reprise (No More Wars)

SUBHUMANS
THE DAY THE COUNTRY DIED

Originating from Wiltshire during 1980, Subhumans was soon to be recognised as one of the finest anarcho-punk bands, releasing numerous EP's and albums throughout the decade.

Guitarist, Bruce Treasure, and drummer, Andy Gale, had previously been in a local band called The Stupid Humans, while bassist Grant Jackson joined from Audio Torture. Lead singer, Dick Lucas, arrived later in the same year from another local group, The Mental, whereas drummer Andy was replaced by Trotsky and the line-up was complete.

Having released a demo in 1981, which was picked up by Flux of Pink Indians, who were so impressed they offered Subhumans the opportunity to publish an EP on their label, Spiderleg Records. 'Demolition Wars' was subsequently released in December 1981 and was followed during '82 by further EP's 'Reasons for Existence' and maybe the one that got the band noticed, 'Religious Wars'.

A debut album had to be on the horizon which is best explained by Dick Lucas himself.

"We were sat around Bruce's mum's kitchen table in early 82, with a list of unrecorded songs: we had more than enough for an LP so had to leave some out, to end up on future things. Having selected the songs, we wrote each title on pieces of paper and shifted them about until the track order was decided.

"We recorded it at the same place as we 'd done 'Demolition War' and 'Religious Wars' EP's, Pickwick Studios in Corsham, Wiltshire. Corsham is a small, unremarkable town but for the fact, it's where the royal family head, down to the massive underground complex beneath it, when the nukes start dropping. The sound of an incoming missile at the start of the LP was made by hitting an upright cylindrical metallic reverb unit, very convenient it was for wartime noises in general!"

Dick continues to give some impressive background on many of the tracks.

"That song, 'All Gone Dead', was the first of five on the record written by Ju, singer of the Stupid Humans, which was our guitarist Bruce's previous band. The next, 'Ashtray Dirt', was also one of his, and remains the oddest song we did, like an anti-smoking song written by a smoker? And played by more smokers? What's that about? Ah, the things you can do with the defiant reaction to guilt!

"Winston Smith asked me, in a 'Sounds' interview we did after the album came out, what 'Mickey Mouse is Dead' was about, and I couldn't summarise it at all" continues Dick. The benefit of hindsight gives him the opportunity to put it right.

"A train of thought that crashes through a bitter society where comedy has lost its childhood essence and reflects in its twisted trails the corruption of culture and mass media versions of 'reality'............. I should've said that!"

Mickey Mouse is dead
Got kicked in the head
Cos people got too serious
They planned out what they said
They couldn't take the fantasy
Tried to accept reality
Analyzed the laughs
Cos pleasure comes in halves
The purity of comedy
They had to take it seriously
Changed the words around
Tried to make it look profound
The comedian is onstage
Piss taking for a wage
The critics think he's great
But the laughter turns to hate

Mickey Mouse is on TV
And the kids stare at the screen

But the pictures are all black and white
And the words don't mean a thing
Cos Mummy's got no money
And daddy is in jail
He couldn't afford the license
She can't afford the bail

Now Dick moves onto some of the songs he has written for the band.

"'Minority' was the first song I wrote for Subhumans while 'Nothing I Can Do' was written in a cafe in Trowbridge on a rainy day and 'Dying World' has a piano splashing about at the end, which was fun to mess about with! 'Subvert City', end of Side one, where the Ramones put 'Basement', a longer-than-most song to round the side off. Credit due to the Vibrators and 'Troops of Tomorrow' for, ahem, inspiring the three-chord progression that is the chorus...a sort of futuristic nightmare of what happens when the 'subverts' get power and its' corruptive influence turns them into what they were fighting against.

"Alongside 'Subvert City', 'No' is the other song that generated a lot of attention, partly with its second line, *"my mother died of cancer when I was five"*, which for those who haven't asked yet (a lot have), IS true. Of course, it is! Who could write that if it wasn't?"

No, I don't believe in Jesus Christ
My mother died of cancer when I was five
No, I don't believe in religion
I was forced to go to church, I wasn't told why

No, I don't believe in the police force
Police brutality isn't a dream
No, I don't believe in the system cos
Nothing it does makes sense to me

Subhumans produced some brilliant artwork for their EP's and albums alike, which is a subject even I can connect to because of the artist in question.

"The front cover of 'The Day the Country Died' was done by Nick Lant, who had done the cover for the 'Religious Wars' EP (after I'd asked him if he could, based on a thin pen picture of a punky head on a letter he wrote). The cover came in the post a week later, gobsmacked we were! He did a few other sleeves, and then seemingly vanished (does anyone know where he went/is?)."

Author's note: I knew Nick Lant, attended the same school and subsequently attended many punk gigs together around our local area. I recall him painting a few leather jackets of fellow punks before we went our separate ways soon after.

Anyway, I digress as Dick continues to explain the cover design.

"The cover/title/end line of 'Black and White' and indeed the whole song was based on afterthoughts and imagery from the riots across the country earlier in the year (1982), a reaction to Thatcherism and the consequent rise in poverty and unemployment."

"We wanted it to be taken seriously, without lecturing people, so typed out the one short suggestion that could most improve the society we lived in; "THINK", repeated all across the inside cover. With an added "ACT/NOW" in the bottom right corner (just in case thinking wasn't quite enough)."

As Dick recalls these musings, he comes across some entries in his diary.

21st - exit Stonehenge festival after a week of it

22nd - record side one

23rd - record side two

24th - mix side one

25th - go up to London to see AHeads play with Anti-Pasti/Adicts/Action Pact at the Zigzag club

26th - mix side two

27th - record the Pagans demo

28th - back to work

"Busy times! And exciting! None of us had ever made an LP before, LP's wcre the most valued possessions we had, and here we were, making one!"

And so 'The Day the Country Died' was complete.

"The LP was released by Flux of Pink Indians on their Spiderleg label six months later and was re-released on Bluurg (our own label) about a year after that. John Loder (RIP) who ran Southern Studios and Distribution was well into helping us out in much the same way he'd done with Flux, and Crass before them, that is he put up the know-how and the cash to make it happen. It was all no-contract, and we took Crass' inspiration to minimise the retail price with the *"Pay No More Than..."* sign on the front."

Dick completes a few outstanding points of interest regarding the cover design.

"The collage of pics on the back includes Rob Challice (bottom left, waving), who was a good friend and did 'Enigma' fanzine. Next to him is Trotsky, sat sweating after a gig in London where the cops in the background had just arrived to check on whatever; that was a line-up to die for, in hindsight, Conflict, Rudimentary Peni, Flux of Pink Indians, Sinyx, The Mob and us. The sideways-on pic in the middle is of our girlfriends living the excitement of the Studio Experience, so to speak and the chap with the mohawk top right singing along is Ju, who wrote those five early songs."

And the rest?

"The rest is history," concludes Dick. "The LP sold a lot, over 100,000 copies, which is mental from my point of view. Oh, and Nick's picture is now on a shedload of jackets....funny how things turn out!"

The Day the Country Died

Released 1983 – Spiderleg Records

<u>Track Listing</u>

1. All Gone Dead
2. Ashtray Dirt
3. Killing
4. Minority
5. Mickey Mouse is Dead
6. Nothing I Can Do
7. Dying World
8. Subvert City
9. Big Brother
10. New Age
11. I Don't Wanna Die
12. No
13. Zyklon-B-Movie
14. Til the Pigs Come Round
15. No More Gigs
16. Black and White

ZOUNDS
THE CURSE OF ZOUNDS

The beauty of anarcho-punk is that the music doesn't have to be as pure punk rock as pigeon-holed within the media. It's all about the beliefs, the attitude, and the mindset. Zounds, therefore, are the perfect fit, and they produced one of the best albums of that time, 'The Curse of Zounds' – a record that still sounds so right today, almost forty years on.

Having played a number of jamming sessions in and around the Reading and Oxford regions, Zounds found themselves part of the cassette movement, releasing early material on the fantastically named 'Fuck Off Records' label.

Founder, lead singer, and bass player, Steve Lake, explains how they got together:

"You know, it was the usual thing. A group of friends who were into music with nothing to do. We just use to get together and play the guitars, drink cider and smoke dope. Then when punk rock got going, we thought we ought to have a band. Not that we played punk rock. But frankly, we had no interest in getting jobs or living any kind of straight life, so we just started to hustle gigs. We played a lot of free festivals and benefits. We met a load of other bands and moved to London where we rapidly became part of the West London squat rock scene."

Original guitarist, Steve Burch, came up with the name 'Zounds' after searching through the dictionary. The meaning is a 'contraction of "God's Wounds"', referring to the crucifixion of Jesus Christ – a mildly blasphemous reference. Burch soon left the group and was replaced by Laurence Wood, and Joseph Porter (who later joined Blyth Power) on drums and the band began to perform many live gigs and festivals, especially with good friends, The Mob. However, it was after they had met Crass that things started to escalate, as Steve recalls.

"We hooked up with Crass when we were on tour, and they offered to put out a Zounds single ['Can't Cheat Karma'] on their label. That was an interesting experience. Our music wasn't anything like theirs, but we got on well because they were a bunch of ex-hippies and beatniks and that was the kind of people we liked. Through doing that record, we got taken up by Rough Trade."

It was this attachment to Rough Trade that led to the debut album, 'The Curse of Zounds'.

"It was my idea to make an album" continues Steve. "I had enough songs and my only ambition in life was to make records and do gigs. Pretty much everything Zounds have ever done has been my idea. Luckily, I always managed to meet people with more talent than me who were happy to go along with my schemes.

"I wrote all the lyrics and most of the music. Laurence wrote some bits and pieces of music. Usually, riffs that I would put lyrics to. Mainly though I wrote the songs."

The album itself was an instant hit in the Indie charts and was also well received for its original artwork by anarchist artist, Clifford Harper. The front cover is depicting firefighters attempting to put out a blaze at the Houses of Parliament while the reverse exposed the hoses were in fact connected to a petrol tanker, therefore, fueling the fire. Zounds was at the forefront of the anarcho-punk scene in the fight against the state of the world at that particular time.

"Everything influenced us" explains Steve. "The deteriorating environment, nuclear war, dead-end jobs, bad housing, corporate corruption, war, police brutality, racism, oppression of women, consumerism, the price of dope. But we weren't unhappy. We used to have a great time and laugh a lot. We didn't give a shit about unemployment because we didn't want jobs. Jobs were boring, and we wanted life to be like the school holidays only going on forever. We were quite immature. But that's cool; I wouldn't have had it any other way."

Did Steve feel as though Zounds were part of the anarcho-punk scene?

"We kind of fell into it by accident. We never looked like that. Not that I was against it. It's nice when people feel the same and wear the same clothes. Makes you feel like you belong to something. Mainly though we were into the ideas of peace and anarchy and anti-nukes and all that. We were entirely in sympathy with that. That was our connection to the scene really because our music wasn't your typical punk rock. I think people on the anarcho scene connected with my lyrics. But then they were living the same lives with the same hassles and anxieties as us, so it's not surprising the words were meaningful to them.

"The same things happened to us as everyone else I guess. We had riots at gigs, got beaten up, got busted, hassled by the police, went hungry, lived in falling down houses," Steve adds.

If Zounds didn't fall directly into the 'punk rock' category, then who influenced them? I was keen to find out who Zounds did get on with and, just as importantly, who they didn't?

"Well, we didn't get on with Theatre of Hate. They were well named. They treated us with utter contempt. I don't like to speak ill of people, but they were so unpleasant and so pompous and selfish that I am forced to mention it. On the other hand, when we played with the Birthday Party they were really nice, and Nick Cave would help me carry my bass cab. We played a lot with The Mob and The Astronauts, which we still do. They are both great bands. And we did endless West London squat rock gigs at the Ackam Hall and Meanwhile Gardens. That was a great scene and was primarily run by some refuges from the Here and Now band. Grant

Showbiz, Kif-Kif and Jonathan Barnett. Those three people influenced me a lot.

"If I start going on about bands that influenced me I would go on forever because I like a lot of music. I guess the key influences at that time were The Kinks, Captain Beefheart, The Patti Smith Group, Can, Hank Williams, Johnny Cash. But there were so many. I liked The Fall and Buzzcocks a lot. And of course, Mark Perry and ATV. In terms of attitude my main influences would have been the free music scene, Pink Fairies, Here and Now, Hawkwind, MC5. Freak bands."

'The Curse of Zounds' has certainly lasted the test of time and I suggested to Steve if he feels it's still as relevant today as the day he wrote the album.

"So people tell me, which is sad. I would rather the whole thing was irrelevant and redundant, and we could all live in peace and focus on making joyous music for dancing and chilling out to. I always believed in a new age of anarchy and peace but I was aware it was a long way off, and we'd have to go through a lot of shit first. I think it might get a lot worse before it gets better. And part of me feels the human race might be on a fast track to extinction. I don't think any other life form would care. But I act as though everything will be healed and better, because what is the choice?"

Steve continues with the state of the world today and where punk fits in.

"The problems of the world are many and varied. People in the punk scene have to do what all forward-thinking people do and work and argue for a world based on peace, cooperation, and mutual support. In fact, it's as important now as at any time in human history. More and more I feel it is a case of utopia or oblivion. I hope the former but suspect it could be the latter."

So, is there a place for punk today?

"There is always a place for music that questions authority, brings people together and is performed with energy, commitment, and integrity. Whether people call it punk rock or not is not important. What attracts me to punk is an attitude rather than a sound. People doing things for each other and for themselves, stuff they really believe in."

He concludes, somewhat ominously, what he thought may happen in 1981 while writing the album.

"We all thought we were going to die in a nuclear war. Maybe we still will."

As I wanted to learn more about 'The Curse of Zounds', Steve describes the thoughts behind each track.

(N/b The following musings are from 'Zounds Demystified' by Steve Lake for which he gave kind permission to include in context with this book).

Fear

"I was scared of everything, even my own shadow. I was scared of being alone with the big crucifix on the wall next to my bedroom. I was terrified of

Father Collins, the Irish Catholic Priest who would visit our home to 'administer the fear of God. I was frightened by my bipolar mother and her violent temper that could express itself in ferocious attacks on me. I was scared witless by the horrific fights between my mother and father, which would sometimes see my sister and I cowering under the table as mum attacked dad with carving knives and bottles.

"By the time we formed Zounds in the second half of the 1970s, there was a lot to be scared of. I learned how the state kept people in check through a combination of tacit consent and fear, mostly fear. Fear of war, fear of terrorism, fear of the lights going out, fear of 'the other'. By this point, I had been busted twice for dope, and every time I went out at night, the Police stopped me. It really was tiring and my resentment towards the police, their thuggish behaviour and their constant harassment of our little crew, grew in proportion to my fear of them."

Frightened of the humans and frightened of their stares

Frightened of the poisons they pump into the air

Frightened of the chemicals they spray upon the land

Frightened of the power they hold within their hands

Frightened of bureaucracy and frightened of the law

Frightened of the government and who it's working for

Frightened of the children who won't know who to cope

With a world in rack and ruin from their technocratic dope, dope, dope

Did He Jump – The Unfree Child – My Mummy's Gone

"While I would never claim anything for my own songs, I think the appeal of this is the same as many other songs that deal with the depressing subject matter. As the subject matter here is teenage suicide, it couldn't be much more depressing. I find songs concerning tragedy and loss can actually be uplifting and life-affirming.

"This little suite of songs is often one of the highlights of our live shows, which is eternally gratifying as a lot of the audience at Zounds gigs tend to like to jump around to the fast ones and this veers dangerously close to the horrors of prog with its dreamy intro, different vocal leads and severe tempo and mood changes.

"The female voice on the record is that of Gina from The Raincoats. The producer got her in as a way of making £30 for one of his mates. Fair enough, I like to think I would do the same. Sadly though, I always thought her voice was too posh, and I found the way she pronounced the word 'masturbate' laughable."

Little Bit More

"I think at the time I was struck by the fact that I, like most people, always seemed to need a little bit more than they had. Everything was geared up to wanting more anyway. Desire was nurtured in the magazines, newspapers and TV channels. Not just the commercials but in the lifestyle sections, the travel sections, the pullout supplements, in fiction and non-fiction alike.

"Maybe that's what is meant by economic growth. Everyone put into a state of perpetual desire for material fulfilment, so the amount of stuff in the world keeps growing. I never really grasped politics or economics at a technical level, and from what we have found out since, it has become obvious that no other fucker has either."

This Land

"Woody Guthrie wrote the song 'This Land is Your Land' and within it described the paradise that the USA could be. But the song also tells us that while the land is in the shadow of 'the City' (financial institutions), with its accent on 'private property', then it is paradise lost.

"I wrote the Zounds song 'This Land' because there are many themes and ideas in Woody's songs that bear revisiting, repeating, developing and paying tribute to. The hope is of course that one day they will be irrelevant and we won't need to sing them. A day that is either a long way off or never going to come."

This street is your street and this street is my street

From the broken phone box where the gangs all meet

To the glass on the path that cuts your feet

To the neighbours next door who refuse to speak

To the cop in the Hunter doing its beat

Was this land made for you and me?

It's your world too you can do what you want

It's your world too, it's your world too...

New Band

"The 'year zero' of punk rock was a seminal time for new beginnings. New possibilities, new growth, everything was remade and remodelled. And it was charted and detailed by the clever dicks at NME.

"Sell! Sell! Sell! That is ultimately what it's about. And in the West, even the poorest households are now rammed with clutter and stuff. Old stuff, broken stuff, new stuff, stuff for the weekends, stuff for this, stuff for that, and everyone's got fucking stuff coming out of their bloody ears.

"Yet no matter how up to date you get, before you know it, something new has been introduced onto the scene and you're behind the times again. Radio, phonograph, cinema, television, stereo, colour, cassette-player, 8-track cartridge, VHS, Betamax, Laserdisc, CD, DVD, Blue Ray, iPod, HD, 3D, wi-fi, PC, surround-sound, a hologram. It will never end.

"There should certainly be a moratorium on inventions. Nobody can cope with the stuff we've got now, so we certainly don't need anymore."

Dirty Squatters

"In the 1970s and 80s, squatting was a necessity. There were thousands of squatters in England at that time, many of them in London. It wasn't a choice; there was no choice. Where else could we live? We had no money for private rented accommodation, and there was no council provision for single people. Local councils didn't like squatters and would sometimes smash up their own houses to make them inhabitable. They would pour concrete down the toilets and remove electricity connections and wiring. You would often see signs painted across empty houses that read 'LEB OFF'. This would be done by squatter activists who were letting other potential squatters know that the London Electricity Board connections had been dismantled. It was local government that vandalised property; most squatters would actually repair and renovate the houses.

"I squatted in a number of places, mainly in Islington and Hackney but there were squatter communities all over the capital. We had a cool squat in Grimaldi House, on the Priory Green Estate in Kings Cross, for a while. It was grimy and seedy, but we liked it a lot. Then I moved up to a place off the New North Road, which is where I wrote 'Dirty Squatters'."

Some dirty squatters moved into my street
With their non-sexist haircuts, dirty feet
Their dogs, cats, political elite
They may have beds but they don't use sheets
Furnishing their houses from the contents of skips
Things that decent people put on rubbish tips
They look quite harmless sitting out in the sun
But I wouldn't let my daughter marry one

Dirty squatters
Oh, my god, they're moving in next door
Dirty squatters
Is it for people like this that Winston won - the war

Loads of Noise

"On the outskirts of Oxford is a place called Cowley. It was one of the homes of the car building industry in England and British Leyland housed one of its main factories there. Cowley is also the location of the Blackbird Leys Estate, one of the most extensive council estates in Europe.

"We didn't go there much. Oxford is up and along the Thames from where I was brought up. The council estate, the factory-work culture of Cowley was something I was trying to escape from. So, for me, Blackbird Leys and its factory world were a bit too close for comfort. I didn't want to be too close to its orbit in case it sucked me in and kept me captive.

"I did use the imagery of the area for the chorus of 'Loads of Noise', which is essentially a song about the radio."

Target – Mr.Disney

"I wrote this on the beach in Kent just up the coast from Dungeness Nuclear Power Station. Everything was Cold-War and CND in those days. Cruise missiles were on the horizon and getting closer every day. This would provoke women activists and peaceniks to form protest camps outside the US Airbase at Greenham Common and similar locations.

"These would occasionally be the focus of massive demonstrations by women who would circle the base, holding hands and chanting. Echoing events like those of 21st October 1967 in Washington, when hippies tried to levitate the Pentagon and held up mirrors to reflect the evil back at itself.

"Strangely, my mother used to teach ballroom dancing to the US soldiers at Greenham Common and other U.S.A.F. bases in the early 1960s. She ended up marrying one and going to live in the USA. I lost a mother but gained a Cruise missile with a devastating Nuclear Warhead. Probably a fare swap knowing my mother.

"Mr. Disney? At the time I thought Hollywood was just the propaganda arm of the US Military Industrial Complex. I think I might have been right."

You're welcome here Americans
We love you but not your bombs
Welcome here Americans
We love you but not your bombs...
Welcome here Americans
We love you but not your bombs
And not your lies
You're welcome here!

--

Oh! Mr. Disney where are you now?
Will good overcome evil the way that you tell?
Oh! Mr. Disney where have you gone?
Mickey's being threatened by a neutron bomb
Oh! Mr. Disney, what you gonna do?
Film's no longer seem quite so red, white and blue

> *Oh! Mr. Disney, how does it seem?*
> *Your films are being shown in radiation green*

The Curse of Zounds

Released 1981 – Rough Trade Records

<u>Track Listing</u>

1. Fear
2. Did He Jump
3. My Mummy's Gone
4. Little Bit More
5. This Land
6. New Band
7. Dirty Squatters
8. Loads of Noise
9. Target/Mr. Disney/The War Goes On

BLYTH POWER
WICKED WOMEN, WICKED MEN AND WICKET KEEPERS

Having left Zounds, singer and drummer, Joseph Porter, moved on to form Blyth Power during the year of 1983. The band was soon to become one of the most original groups around mixing music genre's, with lyrics covering everything from political and historical events to cricket and trains! Blyth Power fell into the unique category of anarcho/folk-punk.

Their first recording, like many bands of the era, was a tape, which was released during 1984 under the title 'Touch of Harry'. However, by the time 'Wicked Women, Wicked Men and Wicket Keepers' was due to be released, all was not well within the Blyth Power camp, as Joseph clarifies.

"I have always been pleased that people have found something to engage in this recording. As for me, personally and intimately involved, it's very much bound up with things that were happening at the time, so it's hard for me to be objective.

"As the songwriter, and someone who has moved the band forward for over thirty years, I'm bound to say that 'Wicked Women' long ceased to be relevant - in fact, it was out of date before we even recorded it. The problem was it took too long, and we went into the studio with a line-up that was about to split, when if anyone should have recorded it, it was the band waiting to start rehearsing two months later."

There are people into anarchy and peace

And others who don't practice what they preach

Some people fabricate the truth with ease

They will convince you that the moon is made of cheese

And when the message is received

Some need a name a cult and then there's some just content to believe

But the ones who are never deceived

Are never believed

It hadn't always been so fraught, though, as Joseph recalls the early years.

"When we recorded the 'Touch of Harry' tape in 1984, there was a freshness and originality to the sound, and it was all enormous fun", and he remembers the first LP was initially due for release much earlier than its actual release date.

"Initially we were going to record the first LP on All The Madmen Records, as it was around the end of 1983 - it was mooted but nothing ever definite.

Then I parted company with them, and the next plan was a very definite indication from Crass that we would record it on Corpus Christi. I actually had a commitment in writing at one point, and I still can't remember quite how that fell through but have my suspicions. Anyhow, time dragged on and by the time we were in a position to go into the studio a lot had happened. There was discord in the ranks, some of the songs had been played to death, and I was looking ahead to getting on with the new line-up. By this time our then manager was also running All The Madmen. Making that record was a kind of sop to outgoing members, and it should never have happened."

For an album, which sold so well and put Blyth Power well and truly on the indie music scene, Joseph still cannot put to bed his ill feelings towards it.

"That recording has dogged me for three decades because, on the one hand, it's the one most people remember, but on the other, it's the one I have the least fond recollections of. People who liked it generally don't want to hear anything else. People who didn't listen to us again and probably assume we still sound like that.

"So, I'm very happy if it has meant something to some people, but for me, the next recording is always the one that's important."

I put it to him that he is being very hard on himself and, as Blyth Power has released numerous records since, it shows that people still want to hear their music and have not judged the band on that one album.

"There are a lot of odd sentiments surrounding the band's history for me - re the 'discord', for example, basically one member was a drunk, and we had to get rid of them. Not something I want to enlarge on in print but anytime we meet, and you want the full story just ask!"

He continues, "Re Crass, a lot of The Mob and Madmen crowd lived around each other in Islington in a housing co-op called The Black Sheep. I know that shortly after Penny Rimbaud wrote to me saying we'd definitely do the recording there were some incidents in which fellow anarcho's did lay into Crass fairly heavily for some reason or other. I can't remember why but I suspect we got lumped in with them and the offer never materialised. It was a long time ago, and it may have been unconnected, so again I do not elaborate."

Stop the city, block the drains
Tear down the houses and stop the trains
And Johnny came marching home again
To watch the news at ten
Cavalry charges in a flank attack
Tape it on the video and play it back
Look there's me I'm the one in black
He tells his new found friends

For me, and naturally, many others, 'Wicked Women, Wicked Men and Wicket Keepers' will go down as one the best albums released during the anarcho-punk period of the 80s. Its uniqueness captured the imagination quite unlike anything which had gone beforehand, and I feel it's a shame Joseph cannot see it in the same light. However, I wasn't privy to all the details, but next time I meet up with Joseph, I'll take him up on the offer of the full story but doubt it will ever go to print!

Reflecting, he offers some explanation for the way he conveys himself on the subject.

"I can never be too hard on myself where Blyth Power is concerned. It matters to me very much, and I am always my worst critic."

Wicked Women, Wicked Men and Wicket Keepers

Released 1986 – All The Madmen Records

Track Listing

1.   Goodbye General

2.   Stand into Danger

3.   Bricklayers Arms

4.   Smoke From Cromwell's Time

5.   John O'Gaunt

6.   Hurling Time

7.   Probably Going to Rain

8.   Caligula

9.   It Probably Won't Be Easy

10. Marius Moves

11. Ixion

12. Some of Shelley's Hang Ups

LOST CHERREES
ALL PART OF GROWING UP

The Lost Cherrees were formed during 1979/80, comprising of Steve Battershill on drums, Dave Greaves on guitar and vocalist, Sian Jeffreys.

Following a couple of low key gigs during 1981, Greaves left the band and was soon replaced by Andy Rolfe on guitar. Steve switched to bass and Warren 'Nuts' Samuels joined as the new drummer. Having struck up a relationship with the band Riot/Clone, Lost Cherrees released 'No Fighting, No Trouble, No More' seven-track EP on the aforementioned bands own record label.

They were soon offered gigs with Conflict and Subhumans, and their second EP, 'A Man's Duty, A Woman's Place' was released on Mortarhate Records and subsequently spent several months in the UK Indie chart.

With the inevitable debut album on the horizon, we asked Steve Battershill to explain the journey from the formation through to 'All Part of Growing Up'.

"It seems that 'All Part Of Growing Up' has somehow become quite a highly regarded piece of UK 80's anarcho-punk history. If truth be told, it was a stumbling, bumbling affair that in the most part happened in spite of itself.

"To stick a tag on the exact moment, it was conceived would mean going back to the mix down of the second E.P. 'A Man's Duty… A Woman's Place' in 1983. It was a night time session at the Surrey studio of Jon Hiseman (Colosseum II), whose daughter Anna did the Bible reading on 'Blasphemy'. The studio was very conveniently built in the garden next door to where the Cherree's then singer, Sian Jeffreys lived. As a thank you to Sian's parents for not objecting to all the building work, he agreed to help us out with an occasional session. We had recorded the E.P. there, and for the mixing process, we were joined by Steve Brown of Jungle Records, Dick Lucas (Subhumans) and Colin Jerwood (Conflict). The latter two were there as both had expressed an interest in releasing the 7" on their Bluurg and Mortarhate labels respectively. This was to be a tough decision for us, but as it turned out, we decided to go with Mortarhate as Colin had offered to not only to do the single but then to go on and release our debut LP.

"At that particularly prolific stage, we were writing new material and rehearsing regularly, not to mention gigging our arses off, so the thought of getting into a studio and committing some of these songs to record was more than appealing.

"We had already recorded two tracks, 'Nervous Breakdown' and 'You're You, I'm Me', at the long-since defunct Crow Studios in Surbiton, Surrey where we held our weekly rehearsals. Stupidly, we decided to use the tracks rather than re-record them, and as a result, a somewhat wishy-washy production by eccentric studio owner Peter Kunzler let them down on the finished album.

"However, to counter that, we also had another two tracks up our sleeve, 'The Wait' and 'Poem', which we'd recorded at the sadly, also long gone Alaska Studios in Waterloo and mixed at Greenhouse Studios. 'The Wait' was a, if not *the* stand-out track on the album due to its vastly superior overall production."

To be a prisoner in the world of the free and it gets to me .....gets to me

Young and female ain't the thing to be, and it gets to me ....gets to me

Hate of oppression in a land of repression, and it gets to me ....gets to me

The need to be different can become an obsession, and it gets to me ....gets to me

"So, armed with four finished tracks, we entered the main phase of recording the album."

Steve continues: "Colin Jerwood had (for some reason) booked us into legendary roots producer the Mad Professor's Ariwa Studios in Peckham. It was early in 1984, and during those couple of days, we recorded backing tracks for twelve of the sixteen tracks that made up the 'All Part of Growing Up' album. It was a crazy two days, frustrating and inspiring in equal measure, the Mad Professor wasn't ready for us and we sure as hell weren't ready for him! He's a larger than life character, who tolerated us for his nominal fee but drifted between an almost contemptuous disregard for the job and sudden, unprovoked bursts of overly-animated creativity. He was keen to record a guest vocal on the reggae-infused track 'Escalation', and he effortlessly brought another level to it, so we were glad of his involvement (he did a dub mix of it which we included on the 'In The Very Beginning' 2CD retrospective). His vague interest in that song was kinda the beginning and end of his interest in us as a band, which was fine. We didn't get each other but got along well enough to crack on with the business at hand.

"Fellow reggae producer Patrick Donegan (Tippa Irie's main man) had been called in to ensure progress, and thank fuck he was, cos on Sunday the Mad Professor had turned up at 4 pm for a session that was due to start at noon, bumping into the equipment causing a judder in the track 'Why Does It Have To Be A Dream?' that remains to this day (perils of recording on tape). He then even proceeded to actually doze off in the middle of a take and neglect to record it. Patrick took control, and we finally got the twelve tracks down. We were glad to get out of the Ariwa basement (recording the bass while sitting on the stairs was not ideal!), but it's something I do look back on fondly as a part of the journey.

"So, with tape in hand, we headed back to the comparative sanctuary of the Waterloo arches and famous Alaska Studios, where we had previously recorded 'The Wait' for the 'Who? What? Why? When? Where?' compilation. That track went on to become a Peel favourite which influenced our decision to include it on 'All Part of Growing Up'.

"The Alaska session was always gonna be far more an exercise in damage limitation than it was a mixdown, and the plain fact is we ran out of time. The last few tracks, which sadly included some of the stronger ones, suffered slightly as we cut corners and settled for the quick solutions to problems with the Ariwa recordings that in hindsight, would have benefitted from a further session."

Although Steve is apparently a little disgruntled that the production wasn't as sharp as he'd hoped for, the album had been put in place and, as he has already explained, it has become one of the iconic anarcho-punk albums of the 80s. I was keen to find out who wrote the songs for the album.

"The tracks for the album, as with the bulk of the Cherrees material at the time, were written in the main by myself. Andy wrote the music for five of the tracks and Sian had chipped in with lyrics for three, but aside from those (and Monkees' 'Pleasant Valley Sunday' cover) I'd written both music and lyrics for everything else.

"The songs, as was quite typical of the time and the genre, were all issue-based. Women's rights and issues of identity and equality ('Nervous Breakdown', 'You're You, I'm Me', 'No Way', 'But The Rape Goes On'), animal right's ('Poem', 'Yet Still Comes The Rain', 'You Didn't Care'), Religion ('The Wait') were all covered. Then instead of writing anti-war songs (too many other bands doing that far better than we could), I generally opted to write 'pro-peace' songs ('Escalation', 'Why Does It Have To Be A Dream?' 'Dream Of Peace'). There were several tracks there too, which reflected the stage in our lives we were either at or approaching at some stage, a kind of youth turning to independent adulthood and beyond ('Blind Or Dead', 'F-Plan G-Plan', 'Nothing New', 'Young And Free'). Perhaps it was these songs and the sentiments behind them that influenced our choice of album title? That, and the fact that it was often levelled at me as a kid that my involvement in the band and the songs I was writing were just in fact, 'All Part of Growing Up'. Having started the Lost Cherrees thirty-eight years ago at the age of fourteen, I sometimes wonder if maybe they were wrong, I hope not," Steve reflects.

Looking for security searching for a future

You save up for a car but probably end up with a scooter

Insist upon your freedom, claim you want democracy

Your lust for independence has that aura of hypocrisy

So you take a part-time job to help fill up your flat
Full of typical this and typical that
You got solitude, privacy and a place of your own
But you had to sell the scooter to help pay back the loan

You got G-Plan furniture and F-Plan diet
There's always someone planning your life on the quiet
Hide where you like, no matter what you do
There's always someone else planning your life for you

The sleeve design was not the typical anarcho-punk artwork of the time. How did this transpire?

"The look of the album was a very conscious move on our part not to follow the more mainstream of the Anarcho outfits. It wasn't that we deliberately set out to try to be innovative or different, we were just doing what we wanted to. Colin had recommended that I meet with a friend of his, Russ White, a photographer/designer who lived in Nottingham, and who'd been responsible for the cover art on other Mortarhate releases, including the second Cherrees' single. Russ was a nice guy who had a vast library of photographs to choose from. He developed his work in a dark room constructed in the corner of his bedroom. His work was very urban, with lots of brick walls, broken glass, inner-city decay and abandoned buildings etc. all in monochrome and all nicely shot, but as I looked through the contact sheets, I felt a bit uninspired as it wasn't the kind of image I felt best suited the project. As I approached the end of a set of contacts my eye was taken by some rather more interesting landscapes and coastal scenes, also in monochrome. Russ explained that he'd used the end of a roll of film up while on a recent trip to Cornwall. I asked if we could maybe use one somewhere on the cover, he was surprised but rather pleased I sensed, that I liked them and we selected a simple beach scene for the front cover image and three other landscapes for the back and insert photos. It was initially received by people with a degree of confusion, but over the years it's very much become accepted as what in its time, was a bold and trend-bucking signal of intent from a band with genuine non-conformist credentials."

So, 'All Part of Growing Up' was ready and immediately received rave reviews. However, Steve still feels it could have been so much better.

"Finally released, following a long delay, in early 1985 on Mortarhate's fledgeling subsidiary, Fight Back, 'All Part of Growing Up' entered the Independent charts shortly after and remained there for several months, peaking in the top ten. Despite its popularity, as a band, we always knew it could have been so much better. It almost sounds like a compilation of recordings collated from different sources, from different times, which is a shame cos there are some really great little ideas and tunes there. But it is what it is, and as is so typical of our collective tendency to constantly revert to rose-tinted nostalgia, it's become by far the best selling and most popular of the Cherrees' studio albums, as well as being by far the worst!"

Fortunately, fans of the punk movement have always held the album with find regard, and it is indeed one of the best LP's to arrive at the time. Nevertheless, this was to be the lead singer, Sian Jeffrey, final recording with the band and, as Steve explains, to this day it was not an amicable split.

"Between the time the Lost Cherrees first entered the various studios to record the thing and its release date, singer and original member Sian had left and joined Blyth Power. Some years down the line Sian, by then a lecturer in philosophy and applied ethics, would go on to ridicule the band in her book 'Next to Ness'. Ironically, when the band reformed in 2004 and Mortarhate released the back-catalogue CD, I received a call from someone at Cherry Red, asking why they'd had an email from an ex-member (guess who?!), claiming to have written all the songs and requesting immediate payment of all and any outstanding royalties. Outstanding royalties?? - Laugh? I nearly shat! This was a Mortarhate release for Christ's sake. If memory serves (and it does) this is pretty much how the conversation went….

Cherry Red bloke; "Why is she emailing me? What does she think this is?"

Me; "I dunno mate, not heard from her since she left the band in the mid-80's."

Cherry Red bloke; "So, did she write the songs."

Me; "Well, she wrote a few lyrics."

Cherry Red bloke; "What? all of 'em?"

Me; "Nah, she wrote a handful. Maybe six or seven"

Cherry Red bloke; "…and the music?"

Me; "No, she never wrote any of the music.'

Cherry Red bloke "You're kidding? She says she wrote the lot."

Me; "No mate, just the odd lyric here and there."

Cherry Red bloke; "Oh, I'll just tell her to fuck off."

"I asked to see the email, and he forwarded it to me. It was a simple, two or three-line message, in which, sure enough, Sian had claimed the writing credit for the entire back catalogue. She had also included an address to send the cheque to, and, her home number, so I decided to give her a call to ask her why on earth she was trying to cash-in on some imagined windfall and chat to her about the band reforming etc. I spoke to a guy who seemed interested as to who I was, but sadly, when he called her on the phone he mentioned who it was, and she decided she was too busy to come to the phone, leaving the poor guy to come back to the phone to lie to me. It turned out she was too busy to talk to me but would call me back later. She never did.

"Fuck off indeed."

Now, a little more reflective, Steve recalls fonder memories of the album and the time it transpired, and so he should.

"'All Part of Growing Up' delivered for us, exactly what it said on the tin. It was a vital part of our collective development, as a band, as people, as musicians, as friends, and ultimately, decades on, as a personal time capsule. Something to look back on, albeit seldom and briefly. It occasionally (very kindly) gets reviewed as some kind of classic. A sort of benchmark achievement. These are massive over-statements of course, but when you listen to it, what does certainly come through, aside from our exuberant and clanging naivety, is that like it or hate it, we were most certainly different from everything else back then, and if for no other reason, I guess that alone warrants its inclusion on the lists of important albums of the genre/time.

"The album, in its entirety, featured on both the 'In The Beginning' and 'In The Very Beginning' CD back catalogue compilations, released in 2004 & 2005 respectively. It was reissued on vinyl in 2014 on Spanish label Beat Generation. Somewhat annoyingly, no one ever made an effort to consult any band members regarding the reissue. It subsequently turned out that Mortarhate had long since claimed ownership of the recordings and handed control of them to Cherry Red as part of a debt settlement, which leads to their eventual sale abroad. An unfortunate, but maybe fitting development in the hotchpotch history of a hotchpotch album."

Lost Cherrees still play to this day, and Steve feels there will always be a future for the band if the sentiment remains true.

"It was planned at one time that the Lost Cherrees would record just four studio albums, the last of which was hilariously to be called 'All Part of Growing Old', but I fear it may already be too late for that nod to the self-indulgent. Perhaps it was never a serious suggestion anyway. What's happened over the years is that the Lost Cherrees as an entity has far exceeded it's original, fairly underwhelming, ambitions. For the band to still be going so strong to this day is a testimony to the benefits of not standing still, for always refusing to settle for what's been done so far, and for never being afraid to change line-ups when changing line-ups is right. Fresh blood. New angles. Youth even."

He concludes. "It's been a long time coming, but to be able to finally feel part of a band which is so at ease with its true status being a constant 'work-in-progress' is both exciting and inspiring. What is clear is that when I eventually decide I'm done, the band can most certainly and will most likely simply continue without me and so long as future Cherrees retain the vision and attitude to do exactly what the fuck they want, there'll be writing, recording and gigging going on, and what more dya want from a band for fuck's sake?"

All Part of Growing Up

Released 1985 – Fight Back Records

<u>Track Listing</u>

1. Blind or Dead
2. Nervous Breakdown
3. Escalation
4. F-Plan, G-Plan
5. You're You, I'm Me
6. Nothing New
7. Poem
8. Why Does It Have to Be A Dream?
9. Young and Free
10. Yet Still Comes the Rain
11. The Wait
12. No Way
13. You Didn't Care
14. But the Rape Goes On
15. Dream of Peace
16. Pleasant Valley Sunday

ANTISECT
IN DARKNESS, THERE IS NO CHOICE

Antisect began in 1982 and originated from the town of Daventry, Northamptonshire. Having performed one UK tour with the then (and still today) popular punk outfit, Discharge, the band soon took on a more anarchist outlook. Things moved very quickly for Antisect as within a year, they had recorded and released one of the most excellent anarcho-punk albums of the movement with 'In Darkness, There Is No Choice'.

The album was recorded at the now legendary Southern Studios and soon received critical acclaim, both for its intelligence and originality. The dark and heavy overtones were somewhat unheard of at the time and the contrast between thrash punk/metal and slower interludes made for an original but brilliant listen.

Guitarist and founder member, Pete Lyons, reflects how he feels about 'In Darkness, There Is No Choice' all these years later.

"It's 30-odd years since this record first came out and the question I ask myself from time to time is, *"Do I still think it's relevant?"*

"Well, I've revisited it a few times in the years in between then and now and, for me, each time it's resonated in more or less exactly the same way as it did when it was written back in 1982/3. For me, it lays out a course for and an outlook on life that still reflects how I feel today. Sure, I might articulate my thoughts differently these days, but the essence of what was documented back then still remains very much at the forefront of my view on life. Relevant? Well, I believe that the world in the 21st century is just as iniquitous, if not more so, than it was back then, so I would say yeah. The subject matter is all still here with us."

The title of the album always interested me and keen to find out more I asked Pete where the idea originated.

"So, *"In Darkness There Is No Choice"* - What the fuck's that all about then? Well, it's an old quote from a geezer called Augustus William Hare. My interpretation of it was that without the knowledge of what goes on around us, we're ill-equipped to make reasoned judgements about it. Ignorance and denial loom large in the way of building any true form of progressive society, and the title of the LP is basically a call for us not to allow ourselves to be numbed to the realities of the world around us. Fucking hell! Seems a long way from jumping up and down to *"New Rose"* at the school disco. It's not really though. If one of the core messages inherent in the earlier generation of *"punk rock"* was *"think for yourself",* this was just a consolidation of that ethic."

Antisect were and still are today considered one of the best anarchist bands since the movement originated. However, Pete has his own ideas on what Antisect are about.

"I never thought of Antisect as an "anarchist" band, as such. For me, it was a lot more personal than some of the more antagonistic politics of the scene that existed at the time. I felt then (and still now) that anarchism was/is the closest thing that might represent the mish-mash of values that lay in my head. The thing is that I also believe that the very nature of our society makes it pretty much impossible actually to be an anarchist in any practical, everyday sense. We're all, to a greater or lesser extent compromised, and the more substantial part of what was written on this LP was an attempt to articulate and reflect the frustration and rage that came with that.

"Musically, back then we were a bunch of kids who had grown up at just the right time for the "punk" explosion to have had a profound influence on our fledgeling lives. We played at the very limit of our ability. We weren't musicians; we were kids who had been inspired enough to think, fuck! Let's try and do something. The ramshackle assortment of bargain basement instruments pretty much reflected the nature of our ability to play them. A Kimbara fuzz/wah? Been trying to track another one down for years after the one that graced the LP was stolen. It's obvious now that it was the combination of crap gear and barely capable musicianship, coupled with a pretty broad range of musical influences and the sheer fire in our bellies that made "In Darkness..." the swirling, raging slab of stuff that it was. I guess also that there was something in there where we thought we might not ever get another opportunity to do something like this again, so we wanted to make damn sure we gave it our best shot to make our mark."

Another modest reply, but I suggest that for many, it was the combination of the heavy yet at times melodic music and the excellent lyrics that accompanied it that made the album what it is.

"A fair chunk of the words were written in the local library. Me and Pete Boyce would often head off there to knock ideas together and see what we could come up with. I remember feeling really strongly at the time about how I wanted no ambiguity about anything we would write or say on the LP. I was concerned that we should leave no room for misinterpretation. I was also conscious of avoiding writing anything that might "date" it and so tried to steer clear of using subject matter that was too specific to the time. Reading back through it, I think that for the most part, we succeeded.

"Anyway, you can draw your own conclusions on that."

Fortunately, Pete is keen to describe each track in turn.

"For now, if you choose to listen to it, turn it up as loud as you can, ensure you are stocked with a healthy supply of beer and amphetamines and see where it takes you."

"And all around was darkness... Like a wall."

They

"A track to set the scene and tone for what was to follow, really. The song speaks about how we have built our societies in such a way that the majority of us no longer believe in them, and in doing so plundered and taken for granted all of the resources that nature has provided. It raises the point that we all too often blame some kind of "external forces" for the ills of the world, ("They") when we should be taking responsibility for our own lives and actions and realising that we too shape the world we live in. We are all a part of "it". The tagline *"There Is No Them And Us, There's Only You And Me"*, was written to represent the idea that we are all in it together. We are all part of the same thing, and in order for things to change in a meaningful sense, we need to understand this and understand that we all need to communicate with the people on either side of us.

"Musically, I still love how it comes crashing in out of the intro. The swirling backwards drums and voices making way to the initial crunch of the opening chords. It was a track that still held on a little to how I had written over the previous couple of years. It still had that simple, thrash element to it, but I really wanted to expand the riffage and lyrical side of it too. I remember how much Wink popping his bass in one part of it really used to wind me up, thinking it just sounded really out of context, but I've grown to fucking love it now. I think it ends in the 22nd round of the last riff. (Count 'em) No reason other than that's where the words stop."

The World's Biggest Runt

"Not its original title. The last word was toned down from something that sounded fairly similar! Guitar and drums intro straight out of the end of "They" to keep the intensity up. As far as subject matter goes, it needs little explanation. One riff from beginning to end. It was the first song where we decided to use a spoken word section over the music. I've always found something really powerful about a calmly spoken vocal placed over a raging piece of music. I still think that section works well with the guitar harmonics clanging about underneath. At the time of writing it, not all of the band were vegetarians, and of those that were, there were certainly varying levels of commitment. I remember thinking when putting the spoken section together with Pete [Boyce – vocals], how much I believed that I would never live to regret the sentiment of the statement. So far, so good. And I can't see that changing now."

Animal for breakfast. Animal for tea.
Animal for supper. "Well, who cares?" (We)
Picture the family. Knives in their hands
All waiting for Mummy to produce the dead lamb
Expectant and hungry to chew on its flesh

Little Sue doesn't like meat. But 'Mummy knows best'

She'll tell Sue of protein because that's all that she sees

Mummy's unaware of blood and heart disease

There are millions starving because there's meat on the table

but try and tell Mummy and she'll dismiss it as a fable

Animals in cosmetics. Animals to eat

Animals fill stomachs. But a life is not meat

Animals imprisoned and engaged for our pleasure

Used and abused as mere toys for our leisure

A Midsummer Night's Dream

"A spur of the moment track and Rich's [Hill – vocals] musical contribution to the LP. It came about during a break in the proceedings when he opened the lid of the piano in the live room at Southern and began to amuse himself by tinkering about with a little riff. We could hear what he was doing coming back to the control room through the ambient mics and asked Barry Sage, the engineer, to run the tape. Typically, not knowing that this was going on, Rich stopped playing almost as soon as Barry had hit "record". A couple of us rushed through to tell him to carry on, but at first, he couldn't remember what he'd been doing.

Eventually, he did, and we worked out another variation of it and stuck it down on tape. Entirely accidental, but it captured a vibe that wasn't represented anywhere else on the album and it was, as silly as it may sound, one of those magical little moments. We decided that it was a bit too empty just sitting there on its own, so I put a guitar part down to go with it, and once the track began falling into place, we added the (out of time) tubular bells.

"Obviously, we hadn't any words prepared for it, so it was decided that we'd write something that wasn't sung or spoken but would be included as part of the lyrics of the rest of the LP. We ended up with both Rich and myself writing something, and as the band couldn't reach a unanimous decision on which one we should use, it was decided to include both."

Channel Zero

"Opens with the old closedown section from the early 80's before we were exposed to the joys of 24-hour television. Recorded by the trusty "cassette recorder in front of the TV" method. The reference to "Winds of War", again, an accident (It was a TV adaptation of Herman Wouk's novel about the events of World War 2). The TV switches to the sine wave tone that was designed to encourage you to switch off and from there, the track blasts in. It's a pretty straightforward thrasher. Again, the bulk of the vocals are spoken and superimposed over the top of the music. Pretty clear theme too. Television – a truly amazing invention with so much positive potential, yet it seems hardly any of it could be seen to have been realised. The song is primarily an attack on escapism and how, for the most part, the emphasis on television has developed in this way."

Yet They Still Ignore

"The feedback from the end of Channel Zero gives way to Polly's tom intro to 'Yet They Still Ignore'. A song about consumerism and our ability to shut out the realities of those less fortunate than ourselves. One of the oldest songs to make the LP. The section after the second verse was added shortly before we began the recording sessions. I remember thinking at the time that I would've really liked to have somehow made it seem like that section had just been spun in onto the tape reel. Almost like someone had gatecrashed the song before disappearing again for the third verse to kick in. Not to be though. Not enough time. Other stuff to get on with."

"It's a shame about the third world.

They're starving at our feet.

Are you sure you're quite alright now George?

Have you had enough to eat?

There's lots and lots of stew left.

It's over there on the shelf.

Are you sure you've had enough now?

Well, you can always help yourself."

(Yet they still ignore...)

The Ghost of Mankind

"The closing track on side one of the LP, and again, taken from another older song. We'd done it this way live a few times and liked the way it built, and gave people the opportunity to interact and join in the chant. *"War is Oblivion and the Ghost of Mankind"*. The "war" that was being referred to was the one that felt like a genuine threat at the time. To put it in context, we were living in an age shortly before the end of the cold war. The British government had taken delivery of the US manufactured Trident 2, (a fleet of nuclear missile carrying submarines) and had struck an agreement allowing the US to station a range of nuclear warheads at various air bases throughout the UK. The concept of "MAD" (Mutually Assured Destruction) seemed very believable. We'd already had the Cuban missile crisis in 1962 and although that occurred before any of us were born, the knowledge that at that time the world stood on the brink of a full-scale nuclear conflict made the present situation a very real threat. The government made, "information" films of the time, like "Protect and Survive" for instance, would make the hopelessly inadequate suggestions that, once we heard the "4-minute warning", we should hide under the table and that way give us a reasonable chance of surviving the nuclear blast. One or two of us attended the demonstrations at the various air force bases; I spent time at Greenham Common (near the beginning, when I was allowed in), Upper Heyford and Lakenheath from where the US f-111 fighter/bombers that bombed Libya were deployed. It's difficult to imagine now maybe, but it was a harrowing time back then, and this track was our attempt to try and get across the cold, stark bleakness of how it all felt at the time. A certain Ms. Annie (Anxiety) Bandez was lurking around the building at the time we were recording it, and it's her and Caroline's screams you can hear as the track reaches its climax."

Tortured and Abused

"The opener to side two, and about as simple a riff as I have ever come up with. Two chords in the verse. Three chords in the chorus. A song about vivisection. We have no conclusive insight into whether other species can reason and think in the ways that we suggested might be possible in this song, but I have yet to see any evidence to suggest that they are definitely incapable of an approximation of that process. The value of vivisection has always been dubious, but that's not the angle where my arguments against it have ever stemmed from. It's a simple belief that we should not allow ourselves the right to harm anyone, human or otherwise, until such time that we, might find ourselves presented with a life or death situation. Self-preservation is one thing, and yes, I agree that it is a natural instinct, but to maim other creatures for the sake of cosmetics or vanity displays an outright arrogance.

"It seems that a great many of us agree that in critical circumstances everything before us is expendable. The arguments can be very convoluted, with many what-ifs and buts, but I still believe that as difficult as it may be to make those choices in a great many situations, the moral answer is no."

Education or Indoctrination

"Bells, playtime, happy kids - another cassette recorder special. No sample CDs in those days. "Poor little Jimmy" is the kid from the council estate. The kid who's background has never suggested anything other to him than birth, school, work, death. Sure, a little fun here and there in between, but ultimately more fodder for the machine. The British education system never taught me how best to express myself. It never encouraged me to examine areas of life that existed outside of what's considered "the norm". I was pretty scared of it till around the age of 14. Then it slowly dawned on me that these people had no real control over me at all. Sure, they could threaten me with detentions and the corporal punishment that was still rife at the time, if I was seen to be "misbehaving", but big deal. They had lost me by then. There were one or two inspiring teachers at my school, but the pervading vibe and atmosphere were such that you were there to tow the line. It didn't matter that you might not have seen any personal value in learning some of the subjects that were thrust at you. Just that you kept quiet and didn't give the teacher any grief during the lessons. No one ever took me to one side and attempted to explain why something might be of benefit to me in the future, even if I didn't understand how it could be then. No one attempted to relate to me. I got a distinct feeling that anything creative was tolerated rather than embraced. We were being channelled to play our parts in the world that awaited us. If we didn't "get it" we were ridiculed as the dunce. We were forced to wear a uniform in an attempt to engender a sense of "discipline". We were told that we should "respect" people that we would see beating the crap out of our friends and fellow pupils. Is it any wonder that the British education system is and has been in so much turmoil? Sure it "educates". Albeit in a very narrow sense, but what would it be like if it had the guts to encourage kids to explore the possibilities rather than try to restrict them to the narrow band that fits in with the ethos of the machine. Of course, it IS the machine. It's never going to offer this. 'The teacher is the system and the system rules your life'."

Teacher contacts Mummy. She says, "I've given him all I can"

All Jimmy wants is freedom but she doesn't understand

All her life she was told that if she didn't tow the line

She would end up just like Daddy and Daddy is doing time

Meanwhile, little Jimmy's confused he's in despair

Mummy says she loves him as he's taken into care

She can't hold back the tears as she waves her son goodbye

Poor Jimmy's disillusioned, and he too breaks down and cries

Poor little child. They've forced him to obey

He wouldn't wear the uniform so they've had him locked away

Teacher knows what's best for you, teachers always right

Teacher is this system and this system rules your life

In Darkness

"Love the bass intro to this. Makes me feel like I'm in a spy thriller. Why? Fuck knows. A quick drum roll and away we go. This is a song about "the masses". As the title suggests, if we don't know what's out there, we are unable to be in a position to choose it, should we wish to do so. We had responsibility for how our lives are shaped over to the state. We put faith in belief systems that are nothing more than elaborate superstitions. We reward ourselves with little morsels along the way. A nice car, a nice house, a holiday in the sun every now and again. They keep us sane, and they enable us to maintain our support for the machine. We are all guilty to a greater or lesser extent. But which is the greater crime? To know that we are willing participants, or to not allow ourselves the moments of clarity to look at ourselves in the mirror. Four verses and choruses. Quick style. Then the bit that went a long way towards setting the template for the band in the years that would follow. Could've nicked it from a Black Sabbath album, but I didn't. It was probably my first ever, bonafide "metal" riff. A 180-degree turnaround at the end of the fourth chorus and Umpteen bars of riffola with the words of the song's verses spoken and buried deep in the mix. The section ends with Wink's "bass solo" complete with more out of time tubular bells before launching back off into the mayhem of the end section. Cue layers of squalling madness before the track eventually falls apart to hang there with the multitracked ringing guitars that herald the next track..."

Heresy

"My favourite song on the album. Again, it's so simple, yet it's always had this seething energy for me. Live, and on here. Lyrically, a stream of questions. Who were we? What was our raison d'etre? What, if anything, did we believe in? It seemed too simplistic just to say that "the system" was to blame for everything. There had to be a level of self-examination and an awareness of who we were, to fully appreciate how "we", as individuals, fit into the greater scheme of things. "What do you offer?" - It's easy to say what is wrong, but much more constructive to consider what could be done to make it better. "How high are your walls?" - The walls being the metaphorical defence mechanisms we use to shut out what we are uncomfortable with. "How long have you got?" - Life can be short. We're only here once. Let's make it the best we can do. "What is the time? - It's the time for change." It still is. Isn't it?"

Hallo There. How's Life?

"Another thrasher. Love the bass breakdown with the weird, circular guitar thing going on. The words, if yer interested, are adapted from Ukrainian anarchist, Peter Arshinov's book, 'History of the Makhnovist Movement'."

"The title (misspelt) came from the kind of thing that people say to you when you meet them in the street. It's a throwaway thing. The sort of nonsense exchange where nobody requires the answer. The shortest track on the album."

The Buck Stops Here

""Is life better than death?" Most of us make the assumption that it is. "Then surely peace must be better than war." True for most of us, but there are plenty of others out there with a vested interest in maintaining violent conflicts around the world. No conflicts = no arms trade. Weapons are manufactured in the name of "defence". Well, the only way I've ever seen a weapon put to use was for the purpose of attack. A shield is designed to protect and defend. A gun or a missile is designed to be fired, to attack. Is it really any more complicated than that? We are constantly fed the argument that it is. The nuclear stockpile is a deterrent. A show of military strength is a deterrent. Are we so incapable of resolving issues that this is what we feel we should have to resort to? "Meanwhile, half a world away..." people starve to death. We spend less than a quarter on aid than what we do on arms. That's just plain fucking wrong.

"For most of us, life brings enough complications that we become so embroiled in our own little worlds that we often fail to look beyond them. The big picture appears so abstract and so complicated that the average person feels unqualified to look at it properly. Hence generation after generation continues to perpetuate the cycle - birth, school, work, death.

"We use the term "Globalisation", yet we all exist in nation states. Well, maybe it's time we reclaimed the term and started to see the world and its inhabitants as a single entity, and one in which we are a true, contributing part. As the last line of the song says, "The buck stops with you"... and me, and all of us. We all have the ability to make our contribution to making the world a better, more egalitarian place. It doesn't necessarily mean we have to make any grand gestures, but it does involve us sitting up and taking notice of what goes on around us and not being afraid to express how we feel about it.

"The track ends on Pete's spoken vocal as the music fades out underneath. Funny now to remember the retakes of the last two words of the last line, "with you". Pete trying to get the emphasis and inflexion right. He did eventually, but it was fucking funny watching him get there. Try saying the same two words into a mic over and over and over again while surrounded by a room full of giggling idiots. Not easy.

"And that was that. A few weeks later, after the final all night mixing session, Polly and I walked out into the bright sunlight of Middleton Road totally wired. Not sure if what we had done was good or bad. Colin was great. He was great throughout the whole thing. Encouraging, witty, practical, and importantly, he had that little bit more experience than we had at the time to be able to suggest ways round little problems, and he and engineer Barry Sage were, more often than not, well up for and willing to try to accommodate our sometimes weird and elaborate ideas of what we wanted to do. It wasn't what we expected it to be. But then, I'm not sure what we thought it was gonna be anyway. Other than an accurate representation of the band at the time it was recorded. Which in the end, it was.

"I still think it's a bit trebly though Col."

In Darkness, There Is No Choice

Released 1983 – Spiderleg Records

Track Listing

1.   They (The Eternal Myth And Paradox)

2.   The World's Biggest Runt

3. A Midsummer Night's Dream
4. Channel Zero
5. Yet They Still Ignore
6. The Ghost Of Mankind
7. Tortured And Abused
8. Education Or Indoctrination
9. In Darkness There Is No Choice
10. Heresy
11. Hallo There, How's Life
12. The Buck Stops Here

THE CRAVATS
THE CRAVATS IN TOYTOWN

The beauty of the anarcho-punk movement was that convention went out of the window and the music didn't have to fit into the 'three-chord thrash' just to fit into the punk genre.

The Cravats indeed testify to this, and their unfamiliar approach had the world of punk prick up their ears, especially after being signed up by Small Wonder Records who had previously been associated with anarchist pioneers Crass.

Founder member, The Shend, humorously recalls how The Cravats came into existence.

"Rob Dallaway and I lived in Redditch New Town, in between Birmingham and Stratford Upon Avon. As always, in such places, there was nothing for the youth to do. Our first inkling of punk, like many folks, was through John Peel, as it was our regular evening's entertainment. We had always been into our music, whether it be Slade, Roxy Music, Alice Cooper, Motown or psychedelia and punk just hit the spot at exactly the right moment. We hitchhiked to Barbarellas in Brum to see The Stranglers, and it was the most exciting, exhilarating event I'd ever witnessed. The next day, we decided to form a band, and The Cravats were born in Rob's kitchen with an acoustic guitar and a pair of bongos.

"We couldn't play obviously but were keen and worked it out ourselves. I took up bass (I thought it would be easier as it only had four strings) and Rob's unique style of guitar playing developed rapidly. Svor Naan joined on Sax (he had various names back then including Yehudi Storageheater and F. Reg), and we decided to make a record. We had no idea how but using Yellow Pages and by trial and error recorded the 'Gordon' single at Outlaw Studios in Brum. My Mum lent us 400 quid to get it pressed, and we presented it to John Peel at a gig he did in Stratford. He played it on the radio a good few times, and the rest is history. We expected we'd be on Top of the Pops the next week but obviously the reality wasn't quite like that, and as we lived in a one tractor town away from the epicentres of punk, nothing really happened at all except we were disinvited to mate's parties in case we acted all anarchist in their parents' lounge."

Although Top of the Pops and instant fame wasn't forthcoming, somebody did sit up and take notice, as The Shend continues.

"Luckily Pete and Mari [Stennett] from Small Wonder Records liked the noise we made and took us on, suggesting an LP would be a good idea. Dave Bennett (RIP), our drummer of the time, found a studio run by an hotelier in Torquay so off we went to England's Riviera for a week to record it.

"Rob, Svor and I wrote the music with Rob and I sharing the lyrics, but it was Rob who constructed the individual elements into finished songs and was the musical mastermind."

The fact that the recording took place in Devon also proved to be the inspiration behind the album title.

"The album's title came from a 'Toytown' sign on a shop in Torquay, and it seemed apt as we were having fun messing about with funny noises, toy instruments and had a fondness for being childish."

Things just could be better
Wishful thinking maybe
Pressing on discreetly
She'll be smiling sweetly
Just around the corner, you are getting warmer
Just around the corner, you are getting warmer

I cannot see sideways
Man is not so perfect
I could die too quickly
Blood disgorging thickly
Just around the corner, you are getting warmer
Just around the corner, you are getting warmer

I was keen to explore the serious side of The Cravats, if it exists, and I asked The Shend of his thoughts on the political landscape at the time 'Toytown' was recorded.

"Well, we were all unemployed at the time (I think Rob was at Art College) and enjoyed being so. You got a pittance on the dole but didn't have to go to work at some shitty job and could lounge about doing whatever you wanted so I never really understood the 'Right to Work' politics of the day. We had no particular faith in any political doctrine as far as I can remember and had a general mistrust of whoever was in power."

As alluded to earlier, The Cravats were never punk in the way the movement was accepted at the time. However, 'punk' has never been about categorisation and I asked Shend that surely that's the whole meaning of it?

"We never really fitted in any punk scene as we utilised humour and were a bit too weird musically for the mainstream punk fraternity. We didn't do many gigs either and even when we had a booking, we would sometimes drive miles to the venue, decide we didn't like the look of it and turned straight back home to Redditch.

"We did play with the likes of The Only Ones, The Birthday Party, Poison Girls, Fashion, Fatal Microbes, The Nightingales amongst others so didn't do too badly.

"We certainly weren't wandering the streets smashing the system and were more interested in playing guitar cricket in the river and creating 'happenings' which were performances for ourselves which had no discernible point. I think it was the love of daDa rearing its ridiculous head."

Dark clouds over western shores, the calm before the storm

Bombs displacing shoppers for political reform

On floor fourteen looking down the streets are filled with noise

Droning voices mournfully accept the celling ploys

Invasions after Christmas and birthdays after that

Who knows what we'll look forward to, mummies getting fat

So when, and how, did you get into the anarcho scene?

"It wasn't until the intervention in the band's life of Penny Rimbaud and the rest of Crass that anarcho-punk registered to any significant degree and even then we were hardly a typical Crass band if such a thing existed.

"We were listening to bands such as Pere Ubu, Devo, B-52s, Swell Maps, XTC and other awkwardness of the musical world as well as all the usual suspects and wobbled along our own path through the musical firmament.

"Recently Overground Records re-released 'Toytown' with all the Small Wonder singles and an extra CD featuring a re-imagining of the LP by Penny Rimbaud.

"I'm proud that every song still stands up today even if some of the actual recordings were naive and showed our inexperience on 'Toytown'. It never fitted in then and doesn't now which is a huge bonus as far as I'm concerned."

The Cravats are still performing and recording new material to this day. I was intrigued to know what is it that excites Shend about modern music and keeps the band going.

"As we still exist as a band and the world is still stuffed with all the hideous inequality, bigotry, evil and trivial nonsense that existed back in the seventies, the relevance of any angry music is a good thing. However, just churning out copycat early punk rock is pointless and boring as music, to us, was always about excitement, experimentation and passion. Luckily there are new ways to get a message across and I feel bands such as Death Pedals, Wonk Unit, Sleaford Mods, Slaves, 2 Sick Monkeys, Nova Twins, Nosebleed etc. are flying the flag of punkness in a way that appeals to a new audience as well as old farts such as myself."

The Cravats In Toytown

Released 1980 – Small Wonder Records

<u>Track Listing</u>

1. Still
2. In Your Eyes
3. Welcome
4. Pressure Sellers
5. One in a Thousand
6. X.M.P.
7. All Around the Corner
8. Ceasing to Be
9. Gordon
10. Live For Now
11. Tears On My Machine
12. The Hole
13. All On Standby
14. Triplex Zone

FLUX OF PINK INDIANS
STRIVE TO SURVIVE CAUSING THE LEAST SUFFERING POSSIBLE

Flux of Pink Indians was renowned as one of the fiercest anarchist bands around, and their opinions on subjects such as anti-capitalism, veganism, anarchy, and peace were as high as any on the circuit.

Starting as The Epileptics (later renamed Epi-X after complaints from the British Epilepsy Association) by brothers Colin (vocals) and Derek Birkett (bass), they soon recorded and released '1970's' and 'Last Bus to Debden' EP's.

During 1981, the band, Colin and Derek, along with Kev Hunter (guitar) and Sid Attion [Truelove] (drums), morphed into Flux of Pink Indians and within the year had signed onto the Crass label. They soon released, what for many, one of the best punk singles of all time, 'Neu Smell' which reached number two in the Indie charts and sold over 40,000 copies.

Vocalist Colin was a big fan of Crass, as he explains.

"We were influenced very much by Crass, and without them, I am not sure where I'd be now. On the one hand, they took out a lot of the fun that punk had been, but on the other, they were the only band/group of people I knew that meant and lived by every word that they said."

Soon after 'Neu Smell', the band were jolted when Sid returned to Rubella Ballet, and Flux was on the lookout for a new drummer. Martin Wilson was to be that final piece in the jigsaw, and they formed their label, Spiderleg Records, before releasing their first full length 12", 'Strive to Survive Causing the Least Suffering Possible'. Colin feels the band were at their peak.

"The line up on Strive was certainly the best that Flux ever had. Derek, Kev and myself had played together earlier as The Epileptics and Martin joined us when Sid returned to Rubella Ballet after recording our first single 'Neu Smell'. For me, this line up had the right balance of political direction and of people that wanted to be in a punk band. As time went on the politics took over, and the music went out the window."

All through our lives we are shoved about

Some of us scream, some of us shout

Some of us complain, protest

While others smile in ecstasy

Why is it accepted as the way to live?

Our bodies falling through one big sieve

We're sorted out, brushed and combed

Some smile, some frown
Some reject the price to how they exist

"The majority of the lyrics on 'Strive' had been written by myself in 1981 but were then added to or changed by Derek who felt every line had to have a political message. 'Tapioca Sunrise', for example, had started out as an instrumental."

However conscientious Flux was about their lyrics and the overall message being conveyed, Colin still remembers the humour, too.

"Even though the sentiments of the album were serious we had great difficulty in recording the poem 'Song for Them', a song about starving children in Africa. The idea had been for me to recite the poem and halfway through Derek would come into the room and start laying into me with how I should get off my fucking soapbox etc. Every time I heard the door go and he entered the room I burst out laughing so we had to record the poem and his rant separately and then put them together."

Colin continues with what he remembers and doesn't at the time of recording.

"I do not have many recollections of the recording of 'Strive', I guess we hadn't yet all moved up to London so recording at Southern Studios in Wood Green was a great experience. Time goes by strangely in a studio; you might start at ten in the morning and finish at one or two the following morning in what would only feel like a few hours.

"My favourite part of the album is the guitar feedback which joins all the songs together, which is just as well as that's all I can hear now, night and day in my ears. For me, there is no such thing as silence. Once the album was recorded, Penny who produced the album, asked Kev to crank his guitar up and create as much feedback as he could put up with. Once done, Penny asked him to do some more, and Kev told him to fuck off, nicely of course. At our next gig, he turned the amp on and discovered it had blown up while doing the feedback!"

We're not very different, we're very much the same

Animals have feelings, animals have a brain

People have feelings, people have a brain

Animals feel pain, people feel pain

Myxomatosis stinks, oppression stinks

I don't want to see man's murder anymore

Experimentation, vivisection, devastation, starvation, torture, war

All mindless slaughter are all basically the same

Man made oppression, man made pain

'Strive to Survive' was another huge 'hit' regarding record sales but, unfortunately, it was also to see the end of Flux of Pink Indians as we knew them, as Colin reflects.

"The line up on 'Strive' was sadly not to last as Kev felt the politics were taking over. We recruited Lu and Tim from Dirt to take his place, from then on I don't think we ever played another 'tune' again. Obviously, it felt right at the time, but it was great to get back together with Kev for the few gigs we played in 2006 and 2007 in London, Bradford and Dijon.

"For me 'Strive' was our greatest work. It was our first album, and I'm a great fan of first albums, probably the only albums I listen to, which is rare because I don't listen to music generally. But when I do it would be the first albums of The Damned, Siouxsie and the Banshees, dare I say The Clash and The Ramones, after that, for me, nothing exists!"

Strive to Survive Causing the Least Suffering Possible

Released 1982 – Spiderleg Records

<u>Track Listing</u>

1.   Song for Them
2.   Charity Hilarity
3.   Some of Us Scream, Some of Us Shout
4.   Take Heed
5.   T.V. Dinners

6.   Tapioca Sunrise

7.   Progress

8.   They Lie, We Die

9.   Blinded by Science

10. Myxomatosis

11. Is There Anybody There?

12. The Fun is Over

RUBELLA BALLET
AT LAST IT'S PLAYTIME

Although Rubella Ballet formed at a gig in 1979 when Crass invited their audience to use their equipment, founder band members Zillah Minx and Sid Truelove were punks almost before the movement was even formed.

Lead singer Zillah tells us more.

"I was 15 when I became a punk in 1976 before the Sex Pistols were on TV and anyone knew about punk style or music. I lived in east London and becoming a punk was a slow process. We made up our own clothes, hairstyles & makeup. Based on the only rule I remember, no flares."

Sid continues, "In the spring of 1979, I was 18 and had been an original 1976 punk for some years. I had just finished college, and I had been accepted at East London University to do a degree. My local was The Bridgehouse in Canning Town, which held numerous punk gigs because of the owner, Terry Murphy's son, Darren of Wasted Youth, was an original punk rocker and a friend of mine from when we first met at our Hartley Youth club in 1976."

Zillah then explains how Rubella Ballet transpired.

"Sid and I are working class punks who formed a band to entertain our friends and ourselves. It was only when Sid became homeless at 19, and Vi Subversa invited him to stay at their commune, did Sid have a chance to play Poison Girls drums. Poison Girls had their own rehearsal room & equipment. We had nothing. Sid borrowed his drum kit at rehearsals and gigs. I had never sung into a microphone before I got on stage to sing. Sid and I never set out to become a band we didn't have the facilities, equipment or the knowledge. It was only because we ended up at Poison Girls house that it happened."

The newly formed group took to the road with Crass and the Poison Girls, quickly establishing a unique niche and standing out from the multitudes in a black combat wear with their vibrant visual image. Always looking beyond the anarcho scene's encroaching orthodoxy, Rubella Ballet assembled a diverse range of material that encompassed all points from perky to doomy, with lyrics that juxtaposed protest and dissent against more impressionistic themes.

Recordings were now inevitable for the band, but it would take some time before the debut album would see the light of day, as Zillah explains.

"Our first release 'The Ballet Bag', a nine-track cassette in a bag with a poster, badge & lyric book, was Lance d'Boyle of Poison Girls idea to create and put out on Xntrix records which were Poison Girls own label. They wanted Rubella Ballet to record with them instead of Crass. As they had given Sid a place to live when he was homeless and let us use their practice room to become Rubella Ballet, we felt we had to be loyal to them. Even though by now Pete Fender had left Rubella Ballet to become an engineer producer in his own studio at Poison Girls house. We no longer lived at Poison Girls having opened our own squat in East London. Our guitarist was now Andy Smith from Flux of Pink Indians; keyboards were Eugene who also played on 'Neu Smell' along with Sid on drums. So really Rubella Ballet was Flux of Pink Indians with Zillah on Vox And Gem on Bass.

"Pete Fender joined the band again when Andy left to return to paid employment. As Pete Fender had a studio, 'The Ballet Dance' single was also recorded and engineered by Pete Fender at his studio."

Sid picks up, saying, "Since the release of 'The Ballet Bag' cassette and 'The Ballet Dance' single along with the departure of Pete Fender and Gem Stone, we no longer had the links to Poison Girls or their financial backing, so it was a long wait before we could afford to record an album.

"Rubella Ballet now had a new guitarist in Steve Cashman & bass player Rachel Minx, younger sister of Zillah. We wanted to record an album, but as poor working class living on the 24th floor of a tower block in East London and employed in low wage jobs with no spare money to record albums, it was impossible. Eventually, after lots of work, we were offered a deal by Jungle Records after we had released a 12-inch single on their label 42F. We started our own record label called 'Ubiquitous

Records' having signed a distribution deal with Jungle. They gave us £1000 for the rights to distribute the record. We used the money to record the album in two weeks."

"Sid took three days to set up, sound check and record his drums," continues Zillah. "We would all play live as a guide while the drums were recorded, then record the guitars and vocals. Vocals would be recorded on the first run through, Sid also liked us to double track vocals, so I would sing the vocals four times to be recorded and played back left & right stereo."

A complicated and convoluted beginning to life as a band but with 'At Last It's Playtime' due for release, Zillah tells me more about the infamous Rubella Ballet artwork and where the album title originated.

"At the time, we were using childlike drawings as our artwork. We were all very young when we started Rubella Ballet, Gem Stone our Bass player was 13, Pete Fender on guitar 15, Zillah Minx vocals 18 and Sid on drums just 19. DIY artwork surrounded us, Crass had their logo, and Gee was creating their Crass art for record covers, flyers, tickets and poster artwork. Poison Girls also created their own logo and artwork. Both bands were a lot older than us, Pete and Gem are the son and daughter of Vi Subversa, vocalist in Poison Girls, so literally old enough to be our parents.

"Their artwork appeared amazingly professional to us, being so much younger we liked the idea of our

artwork to be childlike. We would spell Rubella
Ballet with backward 'e', so we made our band
history into a fairy-tale. When creating our lyric
books, we cut up the Beano comic for comic strip
stories of Minnie Minx. We used lots of cut out
images from old magazines, old Batman, Superman
comics, political flyers, books etc. The childlike
artwork became a theme on all our releases and
flyers. By the time we had the money to record our
first vinyl album, Gem had left to go to take a
drama degree. My sister Rachel joined Rubella
Ballet as our bass player, and we now had guitarist
number three in Steve. On 'At Last It's Playtime'
we used artwork from original drawings from mine
and Rachel's childhood saved by my parents. We
also used photo's showing Rubella Ballet under
black lights which made our home-made clothes
make up & hair glow in the ultraviolet light. Black
lights on stage became part of our show. Crass wore
black; Poison Girls wore red & black. I had become
punk in 1976 and had always created my own punk
clothes because at the beginning there was nowhere
to buy punk clothes. My designs kept to the
ideology that punks were creating their own look
and I started to design clothes made of children's
cartoon fabric such as Mr Men, Star Wars and
Superwoman, Batman etc. Then when we were
finally able to buy our own fluorescent lights, we
sourced fluorescent fabric dye from a factory and
started to print our own fabric to make clothes. We
would use the lights on stage to make our clothes
glow. It was awesome as no one in 1980's used
backlights to do what we did on stage. Lots of our

audience were blown away often commenting they didn't need to buy any acid or that the acid worked well with our set. We have since been ripped off numerous times by other bands and the rave scene.

"As for the title, we called the album something we all used to like at school, and that was playtime, so we called it 'At last it's Playtime'. "At Last" was also a pun on the fact it had taken us many years before we had recorded our first vinyl album and now we were recording it felt so good, it reminded us how we would look forward to Playtime at school and then when it arrived it would be even better than anticipated."

Rubella Ballet is not, as most anarcho-punk bands, your stereotypical punk rock 'three-chord' sound. Zillah expands on how the group writes and create their songs.

"I write the lyrics and melodies continuously as and when a situation influences me. I keep a book of lyrics that we would match up to our music as we created our new songs.

"Mainly it was Sid who wrote most of the first songs by making up bass lines and complex tribal drum patterns for songs like 'Exit', 'Slant and Slide', 'See Saw', 'TV Scream' and 'Trial 13'. Sid had worked with Ray Mundo from Ritual & Death Cult on complex patterns when they rehearsed with two kits. Sid has always taken on most of the responsibility for writing most of the music as he has been one of only two permanent members since he started the band late 79. The reason Rubella

Ballet work well within the Punk community and the Goth community is because of Sid's weird bass lines, tribal drum patterns and that *"je ne sais quoi"* that Rubella Ballet has apart from the run of the mill punk bands. That and Sid's diverse knowledge of music as he has been writing music since he was eighteen. He has worked with loads of artists and written a plethora of different genres from punk, metal, industrial to techno, hardcore, gabba to grime, dubstep, deep house, electro and ambient chill-out, not to forget his orchestral commissions for film scores and advert soundtracks.

"Songs like 'Newz at Ten' was a protest song showing how we were sick of being lied to and indoctrinated by right-wing propaganda piped through the box everyone is glued to, but this wasn't the way Sid wanted Rubella Ballet to be portrayed. Every other band pounding but seemingly easy to listen to drum patterns with phat bass lines, were playing fast Crass style or Discharge esq songs and Sid wanted to write songs that were different like 'Exit' with a mesmerising bass line that wouldn't change but would morph into the drum patterns played as a counter rhythm at around 120bpm closer to the heartbeat than the speed punk and fast Crass songs at 150/170bpm.

"The reaction is more to dance than just to watch because of the speed or just to slam as the yanks call it. What Sid did was to start using complex super powerful vocals with weird lyrics and feedback guitars with FX washing over the whole song. This wasn't standard *"1, 2, 3, 4, Punk Rock"* but a new style of music that appealed to the Goth community as much as the Punk community.

"To this day, Sid's drumming is classed as something legendary and to have seen Sid at the height of Rubella Ballet's career was to witness a legend at work with huge kits surrounded by Zildjian cymbals. To hear him sound check the kit at gigs was to hear his main influences, Ginger Baker, Buddy Rich and Budgie from the Banshees pounding out rhythm after counter rhythm with blistering accuracy and incredible power. Songs like 'Slant and Slide' have a drum pattern that most people think has a ride cymbal played as an overdub on top of a tom-tom pattern, were surprised to see Sid combine the two things played together to their amazement. As you can tell from the diverse styles of music, Rubella Ballet plays that just being called a 'Punk' band would pigeonhole the group and not do justice to the different styles of music Rubella Ballet are capable of composing."

I was now keen to get Sid involved, and I asked that at the time 'Playtime' was released there was a lot of disillusionment around and the country was a pretty shit place to be. What political issues influenced the band?

"There were so many political issues that were influencing the band at that time. We were affected by Thatcher's systematic deconstruction of the country. She destroyed the miners, and as a band, we played as many benefit gigs we could.

"We also supported CND, ALF, Anti-Vivisection, Anti-Apartheid, Anti-Racism, Anti-Sexism, we went on demos, direct action, marches. Our lyrics reflected our views, our band was young and included women, girls.

"Zillah's parents were the two people that influenced me the most because they forced M.P Reg Prentice out of the Labour Party in the late seventies when his conservative right wing views were in total contrast to what the Labour party members believed. This was probably the bravest in party revolt against something that was affecting how the party was seen. Her parents put themselves in the firing line from all sorts of abuse and threats from the press calling them spies and ruining any reputation they may have had. Having to live with the media embarking on a mission to make them the enemy, all they were doing is pointing out that there was a full-on Tory twat in the Labour party. They were brave enough to stand up and say NO even though their name was dragged through the national press they stood by what they believed in and saw it to the end, eventually forcing him out of the Labour party to go with his tail between his legs, so to speak, back to the scum called the Cuntservative party!

"This for me has been great inspiration for my now strong belief system. I believe strongly about the issues I write about and my belief system. We have what to some people appear to be extreme views. I see the things we protest about to be obvious right or wrong situations like it is wrong to bomb anyone.

It is wrong to make people suffer; it is wrong not to treat everyone equally. Basic stuff that is an obvious choice between right and wrong. It defines you as a person, it shows if you are kind and compassionate or not. So politically everything influences us because most of the changes the government have implemented are to the detriment of the people over and over throughout history. So, our songs reflect our anger at the plethora of atrocities happening daily such as governments now accusing their own people of being potential terrorists to poisoning us all with processed food, I mean the list goes on and on. We are writing a new album because the list of things we feel strongly against never gets any shorter. When we were writing songs in the early eighties it was Anti-War, Anti-Thatcher, Northern Ireland, supporting the miners, ALF & CND marches, whereas today we are subjected to bank bailouts, information gathering devises (iPhone, Facebook, Twitter) conspiracy theorist, Syrian bombings and Fukushima poisoning the globe. It's like it's got 100 times worse than it was when we first started writing songs. So, if you read our lyrics you will see everything around us influenced us at the time and now."

Having established that Sid and Zillah as pissed off people with the political farce which surrounds us today, I wanted to know more about how the band came together.

"In our book, we had described what happened in detail when I was 18 and lived with The Poison Girls and gigging with Crass in the late seventies/early eighties starting Rubella Ballet, playing for Flux of Pink Indians but in the beginning, we didn't know what we were creating. We didn't say right let's make some 'anarcho-punk'. We were a group of individuals that all thought alike, protested about the same things and had a laugh with each other. Rubella Ballet wasn't planned at all; we never said before we touched any instruments 'let's start a band', Zillah and I didn't have any musical equipment or training of any sort. It evolved over time and in fact, was coincidental because the house Zillah and I went to live in was the home also of The Poison Girls. I had been to some of the early Crass gigs and was allowed by Vi Subversa to live in their massive commune because I was homeless at the time, shortly after I fell in love with Zillah and we moved in together in my small room/large broom cupboard."

Zillah takes up the story.

"In our spare time, we noticed Poison Girls rehearsing and listened outside the rehearsal room and eventually after the band broke for tea, Dan 14 and Gemma 12, would taunt us because they were allowed in and we didn't have permission. This went on for some time until Sid went into the room daring himself closer and closer every time until he got behind Gary's beautiful drum kit and started tapping at the drums every time until of course he got caught by Gary. After a few hours of begging, Sid was finally allowed to play the drums and then and only then did Dan go into the rehearsal room, plug his guitar he owned to jam along with to the tribal patterns Sid was playing. Gemma always wanted to play, but normal basses were too big for her. Before Gemma got hold of a shortened neck for her bass, she didn't play much leaving the very shy Quentin on bass and the volatile Womble playing another bass at the same time. Pete Fender, age 15, was an excellent guitar player. Gemma got her shortened bass and had the opportunity to play all the time as she lived there. Then we just tried to play our instruments, badly at first but that was the first resemblance of a band, three of us were learning, and Pete already could play as he had the privilege of having an instrument as a kid. So, we didn't plan on being a band, it kind of happened as a culmination of a lot of people but overseen by Sid who picked who he wanted to work with."

Sid and Zillah told me which bands they liked and were influential to Rubella Ballet.

"For Sid and I it was Adam and the Ants, then Sid saw Crass at their second gig, and that was such a change it inspired Sid into being someone who writes his own music than that who follows someone else's music. So even though bands like Bad Brains, The Banshees, X-Ray Spex and the Sex Pistols were my favourites, I still wanted to write my own music without limitations. At the beginning of Rubella Ballet, when Pete Fender was playing the guitar, he admitted 35 years later that he desperately tried his hardest to glam up the Goth style songs I was writing and that was the reason for the poppy sound we morphed into" explains Zillah.

"At the time, at the beginning of the 80's, Pete Fender had left Rubella Ballet and had recorded an EP called 'Four Formulas' after the break up of Fatal Microbes and he didn't tell us that he had no plans to stay loyal to Rubella Ballet even with offers of recording on the now Crass label. He explained his own personal vendetta he had with Penny Rimbaud for the terrible production he thought of Poison Girls 'Chappaquiddick Bridge' LP and therefore refusing to let Rubella Ballet record on the iconic and now infamous Anarcho Punk label run by Crass. So not only did Pete Fender try to change the natural course of the band musically, he refused to let Rubella Ballet record on the Crass label every other punk band was on."

Sid continues, "We recorded the 'Ballet Bag' with Andy Smith and Eugene Crowley fresh from Flux of Pink Indians as I had been playing for them as they didn't have a drummer. When we saw them as The Epileptics they asked if there was a drummer in the audience and I offered to play and stayed in the band for about a year until they made me choose between Flux and Rubella Ballet, the rest you probably know, yeah I stayed with the group, and I started Rubella Ballet.

"Flux tried a few drummers to replace me, and according to Neil, the first drummer was Bamby from Discharge, and I still laugh at what Neil said happened. It turns out Bamby tried his usual speed thrash style, and Neil said: *"No, no, no, not like that, Sid didn't drum like that, he was all tribal"*. So that has amused me, and not a lot of peeps know that bit of Flux trivia.

"The 'Ballet Dance' EP was recorded in Pete Fender's studio in the cellar of the Poisons house, and the reason for the tinny sound was due to bad speakers and dodgy recording equipment.

"Pete Fender, glammed up his performance on 'Ballet Dance' with his signature Slade style solo. Pete promptly left the band after Ballet Dance to join Omega Tribe and record a single collaborating with Penny on production, contradicting everything he had said about Pen's terrible mix to prevent Rubella Ballet recording on the now legendary Crass label. On his confession 35 years later Pete admits to deliberately changing the music away from the Goth style I was composing to the poppy sound everyone is familiar with. I said at the time of his confession that it kinda backfired on him because the gothy poppy style was a hit with the fans and press. Well, apart from our very first review from Gary Bushell who called us hippies on acid and hated every note. Probably the best review ever from the biggest cunt in the music business."

Talking of people you despise, were there any bands you felt similarly about?

"We booked 1919 to support us at the Brixton Fridge with The Mob because me and our guitarist Steve Cashman really liked their Killing Joke impression. However, they complained about the sound all the way through the first three songs and then threw a huge tantrum on stage live, demanded all the money leaving nothing for The Mob and us. We didn't care because Mark Mob said it was the best gig they had done and it was our best gig to date with the crowd going nuts at the end of my drum solo at the end of 'Emotional Blackmail'. The applause went on for ten minutes with everyone stomping on the floor and cheering for an encore. Probably one of our best gigs nearly spoilt by a few prima donnas. We smashed it even with a dodgy PA!" recalls Sid.

Since those heady days, it seems the world has gone full circle. Do you believe 'At Last It's Playtime' is still relevant today?

"Yes, if you look into the lyrics of our songs there are messages everywhere, some obvious like 'Money Talks', others not so obvious like 'Slant and Slide' which was a given point in time because of the terrible state of the world and the horrific state people are expected to cope with whilst their homes are bombed to hell. That's why the albums we wrote are still relevant today because we were twenty years ahead of our time with the messages we are putting in our music, some obvious, some not so but always there, except now when we write lyrics, the things that are happening in the world, the things are so much worse, so much more than most people can handle so most people look away, so we write songs about things people have a hard time coming to terms with like the theories regarding the Bush government and the destruction of the three buildings that fell on 9/11, as well as the attack on the Pentagon.

"Rubella Ballet played AWOD during 2017, and as well as it is a tribute to Vi Subversa of Poison Girls, money raised from the entrance fee was also used as a donation to a women's refuge centre. The fact that there is still a need for women to use these secret centres where they have to hide from men who are their husbands or partners in fear of their lives is a terrible relevant issue that we hoped would have ended in the eighties when we first played gigs to highlight and donate funds to. Animal liberation is a major issue; experiments on animals are ridiculous, still testing cigarettes on Beagle dogs - why? Everyone knows smoking cigarettes kills. Fox hunting in the UK is a major on-going issue. Laws were brought in because people fought the establishment. All political issues have a place in punk because most punks are aware of the issues and the things they want to change in life. Punks tend to be made up of people who still will stand up for their and other people's rights."

To conclude, Sid explains how Rubella Ballet and anarcho-punk really affected the way authorities viewed the whole scene as an obvious threat.

"A couple of years ago, when I was due to film an interview with William Rodreguez, the caretaker of the World Trade Centre, we were in the green room while we were waiting for him to arrive. There were two people there who looked like they knew me and they came to talk to me. She asked, how was the band? I was like 'Who the fuck are you?' to which she continued to ask if we were still living in the flat on the 24th floor. At that point, Zillah noticed I was being harassed and came over and asked who these two people were and they told us they were ex MI5 agents and knew everything about us and Rubella Ballet. They had seen files on us and from when we were hanging with members of Crass and Poison Girls. They knew everything, from Crass to Zillah's parents…everything, and they have a file on both Zillah and me and Crass!"

At Last It's Playtime

Released 1985 – Ubiquitous Records

<u>Track Listing</u>

1. Love Life
2. Tangled Web
3. T.V. Scream
4. Death Train
5. See Saw
6. Games of Life
7. Trial Thirteen
8. Twister

ICONS OF FILTH
ONWARD CHRISTIAN SOLDIERS

W̲e are incredibly grateful to all band members who have given their time for free in helping put this book together. For this interview, Icons of Filth bass guitarist Fish has gone the extra mile and offered us a blow by blow account of this exemplary anarchist band and the making of the iconic album 'Onward Christian Soldiers'.

The following is the unedited interview with Fish.

"The members of Icons of Filth all come from South Wales, and it seems worth noting as this was in itself an influence on the band. The area had been an industrialised centre for mining and steel production. As with a number of similar communities across the UK, South Wales had a history of industrial and class struggle which had seen advances in the rights of the working class made via collective action and trade unionism. Many communities have benefited from libraries and collective health insurance that was set up by workers movements. These initiatives having later informed the development of the health and national insurance systems in the 1940's. It would have been hard to grow up in South Wales back then and not have some sense of these political influences and debates.

"During the late 1970's the conservative government under Thatcher had set about trying to undermine these advances and promoted an idea of individualism and the freedom of business at the expense of workers' rights, community organisation, collective responsibility and trade union organisation. Mass unemployment had become a feature of working-class communities across the UK and was particularly devastating in the mining communities of South Wales.

"There was a tradition in these communities with their Miner's Institutes and libraries to promote political awareness and education. Band members had, therefore, become familiar with left-wing politics. However, left-wing politics did not appear to be a whole solution and looked like it was limited in its outlook and analysis and looked stayed and uninviting to many.

"It could be suggested that punk initially seemed to be quite a mild form of reaction to an oppressive society. Some felt it was maybe even a part of letting off some steam and diverting attention away from real issues while not challenging anything in too serious a way. However, the extreme reaction it got provoked many to start to question the legitimacy of a society that seeks to crush free expression. The smallest divergence to social norms seemed to expose the truth about the social forces that are used to compel us all to conform. The more reaction and coercion that was used, the more punk reacted against this and hence the more revolutionary the movement became. Those who lived through that era will remember that getting stared at, thrown out of shops or beaten up. This was an all too regular experience if you didn't follow something as simple as the currently accepted dress code.

"This was also the era that people had increasingly become aware of the threat of nuclear war. Prior to the band forming, some of us had joined the Campaign for Nuclear Disarmament (CND) which had led to meeting with people concerned about animal rights, which in turn led to joining the British Union for the Abolition of Vivisection (BUAV) which then led to the Hunt Saboteurs and later the Animal Liberation Front (ALF).

"Each new cause led to the discovery of the next."

They'd destroy this world they treat as theirs but say is ours

Destroy us with their wars and nuclear power

Fool us with their lies about radiation

Fool themselves they'll be the remainder of the nation

They won't just give up their atomic shit

They just act bland

Stand up and argue

Make your stand

You're better active today
Than radioactive tomorrow

"In Cardiff, there were a couple of places where you could hang out if you didn't fit in too well, and that was the Casa Gil and Lexington. It was here that people met and many bands were formed. There were some great bands in Cardiff at that time, one of which was The Oppressed who we got to know very well and we had a lot of respect for them as a band and as individuals.

"Icons of Filth actually started life as Mock Death in Cardiff in 1979 with Aitch on drums, Daffy on guitar, Socket on bass and Fran and Tina sharing vocal duties. After several gigs in the local area, Mock Death called it a day. 'Atomic Filth' formed shortly afterwards with Socket (Tony Watts), Daffy (Simon DeManuel) and Aitch (Mark Wilson) and Stig (Andrew Sewell) on vocals. Within a year the name had been changed to Icons of Filth and Socket had left to be replaced on bass by Ed.

"From a music perspective, we had all gravitated to punk due to its rebellious character, but we had friends who played us protest music from other genre's such as Woodie Guthrie, Joan Baez, Country Joe etc. so when Crass came out it was very influential on the direction we felt we should go.

"While it would seem likely that the initial use of the word anarchy in punk rock was more about a comment on the natural urge to desire freedom and to resist authoritarian and oppressive ideas than a coherent understanding of anarchist principles. Once this word had been used many people started to look into the philosophical and practical arguments for recognising the corrosive effects of power and how this underpinned many of the negative aspects of society. Some of us had started to read anarchist theorists such as Pierre-Joseph Proudhon, Michael Bakunin, Peter Kropotkin, Emma Goldman, Colin Ward, Noam Chomsky etc. This was obviously before the days of the internet, and so we found books and pamphlets from Freedom Press and also at the 108 Bookshop, which was on Salisbury Road in Cardiff and the Peace Shop on Mackintosh Place. Anarchist meetings like those in the Urdd Centre in Canton, Cardiff were yet to be colonised by black wearing spiky hair types. Instead, it was a collection of older artistic looking types and a couple of hippies. There was free lentil soup and talk of revolution!

"The Green Gathering festival had also contributed to a broader understanding of many of the issues that the band felt strongly about. It was here you could find discussions and workshops throughout the day about alternative technologies such as solar and wind power, feminism and libertarian theories for change. There were pressure groups like CND and Greenpeace and very decorative radical hippy pamphlets influenced by movements such as The Diggers and the Yippies.

"To all these issues, Stig brought the intensity of his vocal and the insight of his lyrics to bear. From the oppression of the family to the absurdness of the arms industry, his insights into the human condition were inspirational. We owe a massive amount to our brother who is very sadly missed. Neither was his intensity ever that of a performer, he truly meant it!

"Stig had got to know Colin Jerwood from travelling to Crass gigs. I also believe with Ian from The Cult. This culminated in Colin invited Icons to play gigs with Conflict and the cassette LP "Not On Her Majesty's Service" was recorded in September 1982 by Pete Fender at Xntrix Studios, and was the first release on Conflict's Mortarhate label (Mortarhate M1). At this time, Squeelie joined the band to provide his inspired artwork and the scrawly font, both of which contributed immensely to the band's releases. His gothic style art and that spiky font have been admired and copied by so many since. Squeelie occasionally came on stage at gigs to perform backing vocals on specific tracks. The single "Used • Abused • Unamused" was released in 1983 as a 7" EP on Corpus Christi Records. Ed left after this to be replaced by Fish (Richard Edwards) on bass. The band gigged extensively at this time and toured with Conflict. In December 1983, 'Onward Christian Soldiers' was recorded and released the following March on Mortarhate records.

"During this time we were playing gig's across the UK, often with Conflict, and many other bands including Rubella Ballet, Anti-System and Toxic Shock. Various gigs were in anarchist centres such as Sunderland Bunker and the squatted London Fire Station where it was necessary to barricade the doors to keep the police out. The flashing blue lights from the numerous vans outside providing the light show through the windows in the top of the large doors situated behind the stage.

"Although many gigs were in larger venues and were usually very well attended, we survived on £1 a day to get food etc., and typically relied on people putting us up. When this wasn't available, we often slept in the van or the venue. We slept on the stage where we had played and on one occasion on plasterboards in a part of a hall we had played in that was under renovation. We need to offer huge thanks to all those that put us up during this time for sharing their spaces and food with us. It was always very inspiring, and we benefited so much from the late-night discussions that often took place. A very memorable and enjoyable night was spent with Anti System after one of the gigs we played with them. They had a great vinyl collection, and as the evening turned to the morning, we went from anarcho-punk to Lou Reed and Alice Cooper.

"One of the occasions we slept in the van was in November after playing in Birmingham. We had the usual significant amount of guitar amps and speakers that we had to sit on while travelling and also a few people from the audience who had asked for a lift. It was so cold that eventually two of us left the van and spent the rest of the night in an elevator in an adjacent tower block.

"Another memorable gig was organised by Lost Cherrees drummer Nuts. The now infamous event at the Surbiton Assembly Rooms ended in a pitched battle on the streets of suburban Surbiton with the SPG (Special Patrol Group). We had arrived in the afternoon to find a lot of police in the area stopping people who looked like they were heading to the gig. We had got there at about 2 pm, and it seemed there were police everywhere, and their attitude appeared to be very hostile. The SPG in full riot gear pulled up in 10-15 vans outside the venue before the doors opened but initially stayed in their vans. Conflict was headlining, and a number of other influential bands played. These included the Lost Cherrees, Stigma, Legion of Parasites and AYS and Hate State.

"There are many different accounts of what went on that night, but from what we saw the trouble appeared to start with four police officers on top of a man who was lying on the floor outside the entrance to the hall. The officers were holding the man's hair and hitting his face on the ground. As this was happening the vans unloaded and the riot police ran for the entrance to the hall. There was then a concerted attempt to keep the riot police from entering. A little while later the fire doors were opened from inside. This was possible by people trying to leave, although some suggested it was by plainclothes police inside the hall. The event saw numerous people hurt and arrested and was reported as a riot in the National Press the following day. It was also said that a right-wing skinhead group that came to Surbiton to try to stop the bands playing, but saw the trouble that was brewing and decided it was more than they wanted to take on.

"Many of the people involved in the scene in the early days will have experienced the violence that plagued many of the gigs. At one-point, Icons tour dates were printed in the National Front paper with the ominous statement that "these concerts must be stopped". Gangs of right-wing skinheads often made an appearance at gigs. Usually starting with Zeke Heil's during the performance followed by attempts to use violence to stop the band play. Although by this time we had read ideas from Mahatma Gandhi and some of us had involvement with pacifist organisations like the Peace Pledge Union, we often found ourselves in violent situations. I don't think we ever thought that this was a method of social change, it was just a way to protect ourselves. It seems very unlikely that you can beat the racism out of a racist like you can't bomb a population into agreeing with you. The use of violence appears far more likely to more firmly entrench an idea of them and us and not help individuals to change.

"The influence of anarcho-punk was very evident at the Stop the City demonstrations in London in 1983 and 1984. This was billed as a 'Carnival Against War, Oppression and Destruction', in other words, protests against the military-financial complex. These demonstrations were seen as the forerunner of the anti-globalisation protests of the 1990s. Stop the City saw a vast number of different groups take to the streets and slow the capitalist machine to a crawl. There had been a plan for Icons and Conflict to play after the protest, but this didn't end up happening after numerous arrests during the day.

"Touring with Conflict made us very close, and they were all incredibly supportive, and we all became very good friends. We often stayed in their houses after gigs in London. There is a bond that is forged when you spend night after night looking after each other from the violence directed at you from the Police and right-wing skinheads. We owe a considerable amount to Conflict as a band and to Colin, John, Paco and Kevin as individuals. We often jammed with them during sound check, and there was a lot of banter in the back of battered transit vans between gigs. After a gig with Conflict in Glasgow, the police gave us an escort of two van's, a car and two motorbikes and took us to the border of Scotland and told us never to come back. I think we blame Colin for that one :-)

"Glasgow was the only other place where the Special Patrol Group operated outside London. On our return to play Glasgow the following year the SPG attended. We really should have reviewed our guest list! It was also during this time that a police chief ordered a number of bands records to be confiscated, including ours, and we faced local authorities banning gigs.

"In terms of writing the tracks on Onward Christian Soldiers, the music was always a collaborative effort. Usually started by Daffy who would suggest guitar parts and then the rest of the band would develop these ideas. Stig would often come with numerous lyrical ideas, some already well developed, others he worked on once the music had taken some shape. There would be an open discussion about changes to aspects of the lyric and music by all members of the band and agreement as to the final structure and lyrical content. The album featured a more animal rights slant, which was in part due to members of the band being involved with the Hunt Saboteurs, Animal Liberation Front, the British Union for the Abolition of Vivisection etc., and the lyrics to 'Show Us You Care' specifically were a collaborative effort to reflect these interests."

But you don't bloody care and it just ain't fair that
I've got screws in my head

Or if I wind up dead

Or if I look pathetic

Or if I'll get an anaesthetic

Of if I meow or scream for your cosmetic cream

Or if they swap my heart

Or if I'm torn apart

They torment my brain again and again

Or if they swell up my eyes or increase my size

Or if I'm strapped and trapped to a table or chair

C'mon admit it you just don't care

"It was at this time that we were using a hand-cranked Gestetner printer that had been donated to the Hunt Saboteurs to do leaflets. You needed to type out what you wanted using a typewriter on an acetate sheet. This then got mounted onto a roller in the printer. The printer had a large hand crank which was then turned and drew the paper through to be printed on. It was a very messy affair, and ink got everywhere. A perfect time to wear black only clothing. :-)

"In Cardiff, a paper had been produced called The Scorcher, this being the forerunner to Class War. We occasionally met Ian Bone, who was involved in setting up the Scorcher, at gigs and meetings. It seemed that we shared a similar vision of a future but maybe not his methods of getting there. If you consider racism then perhaps we ought to acknowledge that it is not that we should hate the person who is racist, but hate the ideas of the person who is affected by their experiences and has become racist. My grandmother held racist views, but it didn't seem like a good idea to beat it out of her somehow.

"During this time, we played a lot of benefit gigs for various causes and in various squats and anarchist centres. We went on a few occasions to Greenham Common Peace camp on the way back from gigs to offer support. When the Thatcher government sought to bring down the National Union of Mineworkers, we were involved in playing benefit gigs for striking miners. We also set up a number of gigs for other bands to play to raise money for this cause. This included Chumbawamba who played in the Lions Den and the Subhumans who played in the Central Hotel in Cardiff.

"'Onward Christian Soldiers' was recorded at Heart and Soul Studios in London and was engineered and produced by Pete Fender (Poison Girls). Colin Jerwood arranged the studio booking and came along and helped out in the control room. The whole album was recorded on the first day and mixed the following day. Pete was a real pleasure to work with and did a fantastic job. However due to the pace of the work one track was accidentally erased when the multitrack tape recorder was rewound too far. Although we had been told prior to turning up to the studio that we would only need to bring guitars and drums, there was no guitar amp when we arrived. Daffy, therefore, ended up using a bass amp for the recording, although with a little help from Pete he managed to coax his signature sound from this.

"Anarcho-punk was a part of a lot more extensive movement to create change. It helped to raise the anarchist critique that power corrupts. Stig's lyrics talked about the current system that has brought about endless war, fear and environmental destruction. In this time of the internet and alternative news sources, the evidence for this is being ever more available. It seems very unfortunate that an aspect of the anarcho-punk scene appears to mirror some of the least helpful aspects of society.

I'm more vegan than you, more anarchist and
accusations of selling out.

"This could be understood to be more about people
being competitive and feeding their ego's rather
than trying to connect with others. The works of
Eckart Tolle speak about this and how this
identification with your ego can lead to people
focusing on being better than one another rather
than looking for the commonality and connection. It
seems easier to service your ego than to genuinely
contribute to a better world. The basis of Self Styled
Superiority perhaps?

"The lyrics to 'Onward Christian Soldiers' outlines
the blind acceptance needed by those in power to
wage their wars. This is currently as relevant as
ever, as certain groups with huge power and
influence are using various means to convince
people that war and the invasion of various
countries are justified. Some of this justification is
yet again based on denying the commonality
between people and seeks to use religion and fear as
a basis to wage war. We now see a hate campaign
against Muslims to justify the new Christian
crusades to secure oil and strategic dominance
across the world. The manipulation of news and the
use of false flag operations give an indication as to
how much certain groups want perpetual war. Stig's
lyric's in 'Fool Britannia' yet again appear
extremely relevant to our current situation where
big multinationals benefit from selling arms and

then benefit still from rebuilding the countries their arms destroyed.

There is a war to create fear.

"Stig's lyrics spoke of the indoctrination and expectation of our society to conform to its ideas. We know how quickly people can be influenced to change their behaviour from history and the social sciences. The Stanford prison experiment and what we saw in Nazi Germany give clear examples. Imagine that world we can create if we develop a society that is based on empathy and cooperation rather than self-interest and competition.

Evolve or die.

"Many things have changed positively since the early days of anarcho-punk. It would be nice to think that the anarcho-punk movement made some contribution to this. There are certainly a lot of people within the scene who are very informed and work hard to live in a way that contributes to moving things forward. But it seems sensible to accept that we were all fortunate to have had the life experiences (no matter how hard attained) that allowed us to start to better develop our empathy and our ability to envisage a better world.

Connection, not competition.

"Since the 1980s there have been considerable advances in human understanding such as that in the neuroscience, psychology, biology and the sociological understanding of the world. There is now a vast wealth of evidence about the neuroplasticity of the human brain and our ability for the brain to enhance specific attributes according to its environment. Not only are our brains affected by our environment but our beliefs are affected by it also. If therefore we have a society based on competition, then our brains will focus our abilities in that area and take resources away from other abilities. Children are less affected by this environmental conditioning and hence can occasionally see through this blinkered thinking. When he wrote the lyrics to 'Sod The Children', Stig obviously wanted to point out how this conditioning can so often blind adults to the truth. Given that the human brain adapts to its environment, maybe this understanding provides yet more compelling evidence, not vilify the person who is more easily drawn to engage in actions or hold beliefs that appear oppressive to the person themselves or others. Examples of this could be drug addiction, violent behaviour, through to racist and homophobic ideas. Similarly, it seems sensible that we can't blame an individual who has developed capitalist ideas in an environment that has perpetuated the myths of difference, self-interest and competition. Those people have not been at all fortunate.

Beware the beliefs that created the past.

"The world will always need voices to speak out for positive change and music is one of the methods for helping people both to connect and to share ideas. It seems sad that there has been a part of the anarcho-punk scene that is characterised by accusations about people's failings rather than their strengths. The movement for freedom of expression seems to have turned in on itself with accusations of selling out and I'm more right / right on than you. Eckhart Tolle suggests that people's ego drives this type of behaviour and that their ego fools them into thinking that they can feel better by pointing out the failings of others. Of course, it is healthy to be critical of issues, but research indicates that it is so much more productive to use praise to encourage individuals to change rather than use criticism. Meanwhile being right at the expense of your connection and empathy with others seems to be taking steps along the road to war.

Nothing is more oppressive than a cherished belief.

"Stig's lyric in 'Why So Limited' alluded to the limitations that we place on ourselves and that humankind is so often constrained and held hostage by the current belief system. A look at current issues around the world, however, indicates huge concerns that the system we have is broken. Mainstream beliefs have created a system that is wrecking the environment, undermine our health and our relationships with one another by nurturing competition and self-interest. It would seem that unless we move away from individuals being controlled by their own ego's, then we are unlikely to be able to move away from a society based on this self-interest and competition and ultimate devastation.

"If we truly want freedom, equity and peace then we need to look within ourselves first. Although there is an ever-increasing number of people, who are embracing more enlightened thinking it is obvious that there is still a long way to go. Recent events in politics, boom and bust capitalism, invasions of various countries, the war to create terror and the manipulation of the news are all good examples of a system which is corrupt and failing. It is therefore very sad to find that over 30 years on and Stig's lyrics on 'Onward Christian Soldiers' are as revealing, relevant and insightful as they ever were, about a world that needs to evolve. His memory will always be with us, and his lyrics will forever inspire."

"Change is inevitable, but choice requires action.

Better active today."

Onward Christian Soldiers

Released 1984 – Mortarhate Records

Track Listing

1.   Why So Limited?

2.   Mentally Murdered

3.   They've Taken Everything

4. Fucked Up State

5. Present and History

6. Dividing Line

7. Now We're Getting Warmer

8. Sod The Children

9. Show Us You Care

10. Death Is The Only Reason

11. Fool Britannia (A Song For Europe)

12. One Second To Midnight

13. Onward Christian Soldiers

14. Self-Styled Superiority

15. Power For Power

DEDICATIONS AND ACKNOWLEDGEMENTS

Dedicated to all our readers at www.punkonline.co.uk and all our contributors who have made the website a huge success.

Also to all the punks who continue to believe that we don't merely have to conform to the status quo and there is an alternative if we just think.

My heartfelt thanks to everybody who contributed to making this book possible. The individuals from the bands, who gave their time for free and never once complained about my persistent emails. They have made this book possible and without their input and let's face it, without their music, there wasn't even any subject matter, to begin with.

Please support these bands, whether they are still playing to this day or not. All the albums featured are available to purchase from one place or another, and I can personally vouch that they sound as good today as they did in the 80s.

Maybe a sad reflection on the state of the world, but they are all still just as relevant.

Printed in Poland
by Amazon Fulfillment
Poland Sp. z o.o., Wrocław